CROSS STITCH
COUNTRY CHRISTMAS

CROSS STITCH
COUNTRY CHRISTMAS

BRENDA KEYES

*Running to the window, he opened it and put out his head.
No fog, no mist; clear, bright, jovial, stirring, cold; cold,
piping for the blood to dance to; Golden sunlight; Heavenly
sky; sweet fresh air; merry bells. Oh, glorious, Glorious!*

*"What's to-day, my fine fellow?" cried Scrooge, calling
downward to a boy in Sunday clothes, who perhaps had
loitered in to look about him.*

"EH?" returned the boy, with all his might of wonder.

"What's today my fine fellow?" said Scrooge.

"To-day!" replied the boy. "Why, CHRISTMAS DAY."

A Christmas Carol CHARLES DICKENS 1843

David & Charles

For my children Katie and Nicholas, who
love Christmas almost as much as I do

A DAVID & CHARLES BOOK
Copyright © Text, charts and designs Brenda Keyes 1994, 1996
Photography and layout Copyright © David & Charles 1994, 1996
First published 1994
First paperback edition 1996

Brenda Keyes has asserted her right to be identified as author of this work in
accordance with the Copyright, Designs and Patents Act 1988.

A catalogue record for this book is available from the British Library.

ISBN 0 7153 0532 8

Typeset by ICON Graphic Services
and printed in Italy by LEGO SpA, Vicenza
for David & Charles
Brunel House Newton Abbot Devon

CONTENTS

* * * * * * * * *

INTRODUCTION

✱ ✱ ✱ ✱ ✱ ✱ ✱ ✱ ✱ ✱ ✱

Writing this book has been great fun. I am sure many people would have doubts about their continued enthusiasm for the festive season were it to extend not only into January and February, but also to consume their lives for 365 days of the year. I am happy to report, however, that immersing myself in 'all things Christmas' for the last twelve months has done nothing to dull my enthusiasm for what is, and shall always remain, my favourite time of the year.

I sincerely hope that the projects in this book will inspire the reader to take up needle and thread and either stitch something for their home that will delight them for many years to come; or perhaps take a fresh look at the art of present giving and take the time and trouble to make a uniquely personal offering which will be admired and treasured. It is no accident that many of the items in the book feature sampler motifs and alphabets, for they are (as you will know if you have my last book, *Alphabets & Samplers*) my raison d'être! A personalised gift with initials or a name is sure to be treasured, so I have included an alphabets and numerals page.

The projects themselves are wide and varied. They range from tiny sampler-motif tree ornaments framed with ice-lolly sticks to resemble 'cross-corner' frames, to the more detailed and time-consuming items, such as the Advent Calendar or the Merry Christmas Around the World hoop. Most of the small projects are ideal 'stall-fillers' for that ever looming Christmas fair – a varied selection of the tree ornaments and small gifts would make an attractive display if grouped together.

Throughout the book there are further suggestions for using the designs and I very much hope that you will go on to invent many more ideas of your own. Whichever projects you choose to make or adapt, I hope that stitching them will bring you as much joy as it has for me!

Brenda Keyes 1993

WORKBOX

The projects in this book all use the technique of counted cross stitch, where the design is worked from a chart rather than being printed on fabric or canvas. The technique involved in 'reading' the chart and then 'translating' it to the fabric is an easy one to master and, once understood, will open up a host of exciting possibilities. Not only will you be able to work from any counted cross stitch chart, but you will also find it easy to adapt, enlarge, reduce and eventually create designs of your own easily and quickly.

Understanding Charts

There are many different types of charts – black and white, coloured, hand-drawn, computer generated, coloured squares or symbols, or coloured squares with symbols. Fear not! The method for 'translating' all of them is the same. One square on the chart, containing a symbol or colour, represents one stitch (usually a cross stitch) on your fabric. Figure 1 shows clearly how the chart has been 'translated' on to the fabric.

The blank squares on your chart mean that this area is unworked (one very good reason for the huge popularity of counted cross stitch – no unending acres of beige to fill in!). The straight black lines surrounding a motif indicate back stitch. They will add impact to your design and will often help to define areas that would otherwise blend into each other. Black is usually suggested for outlining but is sometimes too harsh, in which case a softer shade of grey or brown, or any darker shade of a colour already used is more appropriate. Unless the design is worked in one colour only, a key will be given on the chart to indicate which colours to use for each stitch.

Threads

The vast range of threads available to the stitcher today, offered in an enormous choice of colours, means almost unlimited design possibilities. The most commonly used thread for counted cross stitch is stranded cotton (floss). It is treated by a process known as mercerisation, which gives it a polished sheen like silk. The advantage of stranded cotton is that the strands can be separated and recombined in any number to achieve different effects. As the cotton (floss) has six strands, many variations are possible. Two strands are commonly used for cross stitch, although one strand is used over one thread of

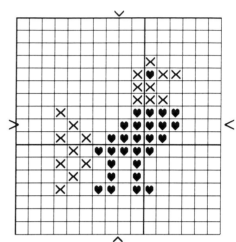

Fig 1 Chart of Bird Motif

fabric to create delicate effects, or to give emphasis when outlining in back stitch.

There is no reason to limit yourself to the sole use of stranded cotton (floss). Wonderful effects can be achieved by substituting different threads. Try experimenting with threads you may not have used before – perlé cotton, flower threads, metallic thread, fine wool, viscose rayon thread – the list is endless. A somewhat ordinary piece of work can be totally transformed by the substitution or addition of some of the more unusual threads.

Perlé cotton is a highly mercerised, twisted, non-divisible, lustrous cotton thread available in a skein or a ball. Crewel wool is a very fine, smooth, 2-ply wool. Flower thread is a non-divisible matt-finish thread made of 100 per cent cotton. DMC Laine Colbert is a superior quality, non-divisible, 4-ply wool which is moth-proof and colourfast. Madeira Decor is a lustrous rayon thread, which is soft, smooth and shiny – perfect for making tassels. Marlitt is a 4-ply viscose rayon thread with a high sheen.

The projects in this book use DMC stranded cotton (floss) unless otherwise specified. There is a DMC to Anchor conversion chart on page 125 for those who wish to use Anchor threads. All perlé cottons used are No 5.

Using Space-dyed or Variegated Thread

Wonderful effects can be achieved if these threads are used sympathetically. A simple design (an alphabet or name for example) can be transformed by substituting this type of thread for a single colour. When using variegated thread (where the colour gradually changes from a very pale to a dark shade of the same colour), it is important to select the lengths so that the gradual change of colour is followed throughout your stitching, ie do not place dark thread next to light. Beautifully subtle effects can be achieved if the colours merge gradually. On the other hand, some space-dyed threads are dyed with sudden and dramatic changes of colour at very short intervals, giving a totally different look.

For both types of thread, it is important to complete each cross stitch individually, and not work a line of half crosses and then complete by working back along the line.

Thread Storage

Storing your threads in an organised and efficient manner will enable you to see and select threads at a glance. There are many methods of thread storage, ranging from cards with holes punched in them to hold cut skeins, storage boxes with cards to wrap thread around, and sophisticated thread organisers that store threads in plastic pockets which are then housed in a binder. Whichever method you choose (including your own versions of the above), storing your threads carefully will ensure that they are clean and tangle free. They are after all, the artist's palette from which all your creations will emerge!

Needles

You will need blunt tapestry needles for all types of counted needlework. The most commonly used sizes are 22, 24 and 26. The size selected will depend on the fabric used. For example size 22 for 8-count Aida, size 26 for fine 30- to 36-count linen. The needle should offer a little pressure when passed through the fabric, and should not be able to drop right through the hole. Always try to keep at least one packet of each size of needle in stock, as it is infuriating not to be able to start your project for lack of the appropriate needle.

Fabrics

Counted needlework requires an evenweave fabric, that is, a fabric that has the same number of threads horizontally as vertically. Such fabrics are described by the number of threads or blocks per inch (25mm) usually known as the count. This count will determine the finished size of the design.

A wonderful variety of evenweave fabrics is now available for counted needlework, with two main types – Aida and linen. Aida fabrics are constructed in blocks, which makes counting easier and prevents uneven stitching, especially for beginners.

Various types of Aida and linen fabric have been used in the following projects. Aida fabrics include: Ainring, which is woven to form blocks of four threads, with 18 blocks to the inch (25mm); Rustico, available in 14- or 18-count, is a naturally woven cotton fabric with a country feel; Hardanger is a cotton fabric woven with pairs of threads, usually 22 pairs to the inch (25mm).

Linen fabrics include: Edinburgh linen, a 36-count, high quality linen; Belfast linen, of similar quality but in 32-count; Dublin linen, a 25-count linen woven from fine quality flax; and Cork linen, a 19-count linen, made from strong, bleached flax.

Aida, linen and other fabrics, such as plastic and perforated paper, are available in a wide range of colours. Do try experimenting – you need not restrict yourself to the usual white, cream or beige. Many of the projects in this book have been worked on wonderful 'Christmassy' colours – red, dark green and navy blue, which provide a striking background to the design. (This highlights the advantage of cross stitch as opposed to needlepoint; you stitch the interesting part, not large areas of background!)

Fabric Allowance

It is essential to allow enough fabric surrounding the design area for stretching and framing. As a general rule, 4–6in (102–152mm) will be sufficient, although smaller pieces such as brooches, miniatures and cards will not require this much excess. The information on page 10 shows how to calculate the amount of fabric required for a design (or alternative fabrics with different thread counts). Once you have mastered the technique of calculating in this way you will find it an easy task to select the correct amount of fabric required for counted work.

Always measure your fabric carefully and cut along a thread line using sharp dressmaking scissors. There are a number of methods you can use to prevent the cloth from fraying: oversew the edges by hand; machine the edges using a zig-zag stitch; bind the edges with tape (*not* masking tape as it can pull threads when being removed and also leave a sticky residue); or use a commercially made material called Fray-check, which is applied to the edges of fabric.

Calculating Quantities of Alternative Fabrics

Cross Stitching on Linen over Two Threads
For example: 25 threads per inch linen with design area 100 stitches high × 50 wide. Divide the number of vertical stitches in the design area by the stitch count of the fabric and multiply by 2. This will give you the size of the design area in inches (or millimetres). Repeat this procedure for the horizontal stitches.

Thus:

$$\frac{100}{25} = 4 \times 2 = 8\text{in (203mm)}$$

$$\frac{50}{25} = 2 \times 2 = 4\text{in (102mm)}$$

So the design area is 8 × 4in (203 × 102mm). Add 4–6in (102–152mm) for finishing, and the fabric required is 12 × 8in (305 × 203mm).

Cross Stitching on 'Block' Fabrics such as Aida or Over One Thread of Linen
For example: 10-count Aida with design area 100 stitches high × 50 wide. Divide the number of vertical stitches in the design area by the stitch count of the fabric and this will give you the size of the design area in inches (or millimetres). Repeat this procedure for the horizontal stitches.

Thus:

$$\frac{100}{10} = 10\text{in (254mm)}$$

$$\frac{50}{10} = 5\text{in (127mm)}$$

So the design area is 10 × 5in (254 × 127mm). Add 4–6in (102–152mm) for finishing, and the fabric required is 14 × 9in (356 × 229mm).

Hoops and Frames

If you decide to use an embroidery hoop – and they can be a very helpful aid to accurate stitching – always use one that is big enough to house the complete design comfortably. This will ensure that the hoop never needs to be placed over any stitching and will thus avoid spoiling the completed work with pulled and snagged stitches. To prevent your fabric slipping about, it is advisable to bind the inner hoop with white bias binding secured with a few stitches.

Another way to protect your work from hoop marks is to place a piece of tissue paper between the fabric and hoop then tear away the middle section to expose the area to be worked. Hoops tend to leave crease marks that are almost impossible to remove, so always remember to remove the hoop every time you finish working.

Larger pieces of work will require a rectangular frame. They come in many sizes including large free-standing floor frames. Some have the added benefit of a magnifying light. After the side edges of the fabric have been bound with tape or hemmed to strengthen them, the top and bottom edges of the fabric are sewn to the webbing which is attached to the rollers of the frame. It is important to ensure that the fabric is placed evenly in the frame, as if it is sewn in unevenly it will become distorted. The frame is then assembled and the side edges laced to the stretchers with very strong thread (see Figure 2).

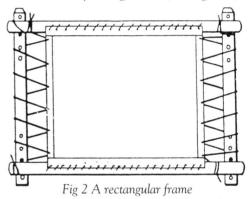

Fig 2 A rectangular frame

A quicker and easier, though just as effective, way of keeping your fabric taut, is to use ready-made rectangular frames which are available in a variety of sizes from some embroidery shops. The fabric is stapled straight on to the frame (or attached with drawing pins), thus saving a great deal of time and effort. Although less elegant than roller frames, I feel they have many advantages – there are no protruding corners to catch your thread on, they are lighter to hold, easier to store and more portable. For really large pieces of work however, where the overall size would rule out the possibility of holding the entire framed piece comfortably, a roller frame would be more appropriate.

Enlarging and Reducing Charted Designs

Charted designs are extremely versatile and very easy to enlarge or reduce in size. For example, a small motif could be enlarged, using the method described opposite, to use as a panel for a cushion. Alternatively, a large, elaborate initial (see Elegant

Alphabet pages 108–18) could easily be reduced in size to fit a tiny brooch. There are a number of ways to do this.

1 Consider every square in the design to be two, three or even four stitches square instead of one. For example, to triple the design size, work a block of stitches three by three for every *one* stitch shown.

2 Work the stitches over two, three or even four threads or blocks of fabric (Aida commonly). For example, if you work over four threads instead of two, the design will double in size. Likewise, if the instructions state that the design is worked in cross stitch over two threads of linen and you work over just one thread in either cross stitch or tent stitch, the design size will be halved.

3 The fabric chosen will also play a large part in determining the size of the design. For example, working over one block of 11-count Aida as opposed to working the same design over one thread of linen 36 threads per inch (25 mm), will increase the design size dramatically.

How to Begin Working

Finding the centre of the fabric
Fold your fabric in half and half again and crease lightly. Tack (baste) along these lines in a contrasting sewing thread. The centre of the fabric is where the lines cross. Most instructions suggest that you begin work at this point – this is to ensure that your work is distributed evenly, avoiding the horrible possibility of working off the edge of the fabric! However, if you want to start work at, say, the top left-hand corner of the design (and this does seem to be a more logical alternative with designs that include a border), you must carefully calculate where to start by deducting the design size from your fabric size and positioning accordingly. For example, if your fabric size is 12 × 10in (305 × 254mm) and your design size 8 × 6in (203 × 152mm), you will have 4in (102mm) of spare fabric. You should therefore measure 2in (51mm) down from the top edge and 2in (51mm) in from the side edge and begin work here.

Starting to Stitch
The following list of do's and don'ts will ensure that you achieve a perfect start and a perfect finish.

1 Cut your thread no longer than 12–18in (305–457mm).

2 When using stranded cotton (floss), always separate and untwist all six strands before selecting the number of strands required. (The amount will depend on the fabric used.) This method will ensure that the threads lie flatter and give greater coverage.

3 Never use a knot to begin stitching because knots can pull through and will give a bumpy finish which will spoil the appearance of your work. To begin stitching on previously unworked fabric, bring the needle up through the fabric leaving about an inch (25mm) of thread at the back. Holding this thread in place, work three or four stitches until the trailing thread is caught and secured. To begin a new thread on fabric which has been previously stitched, simply run the needle through the loops of three or four stitches at the back of the work near to where you wish to begin stitching. Bring the needle up at the required place, and begin.

4 Be careful not to pull stitches too tightly. They should sit evenly on the fabric – tension is just as important in embroidery as in knitting.

5 Make sure that all top stitches in cross stitch are in the same direction to ensure a smooth, even finish.

6 Remember to 'drop' your needle every four or five stitches. This will take the twist out of the thread and avoid tangles.

7 The method for finishing/securing a thread is much the same as starting. Leaving yourself enough thread to finish, take the needle through to the back of the work. Run the needle through the back loop of three or four stitches and snip off the thread close to the stitching.

Working the Project
Stitch instructions are given in the Stitch Directory (page 120). Further skills, such as finishing, mounting and framing a completed piece of embroidery, making a hoop frill, making a fold-over card, or a twisted cord and tassels, are described at the back of the book (see Finishing Techniques pages 121–24). For suppliers of the materials used, refer to Acknowledgements on page 127.

A PARTRIDGE IN A PEAR TREE

Inspired by the words of the popular song, this simple yet effective design of a partridge in a pear tree is worked in cross stitch using two strands of cotton (floss) over one block of Yorkshire Aida fabric, which gives it a wonderful country feel.

Design size: 5¼ × 4½in (133 × 114mm)
Stitch count: 73 × 62

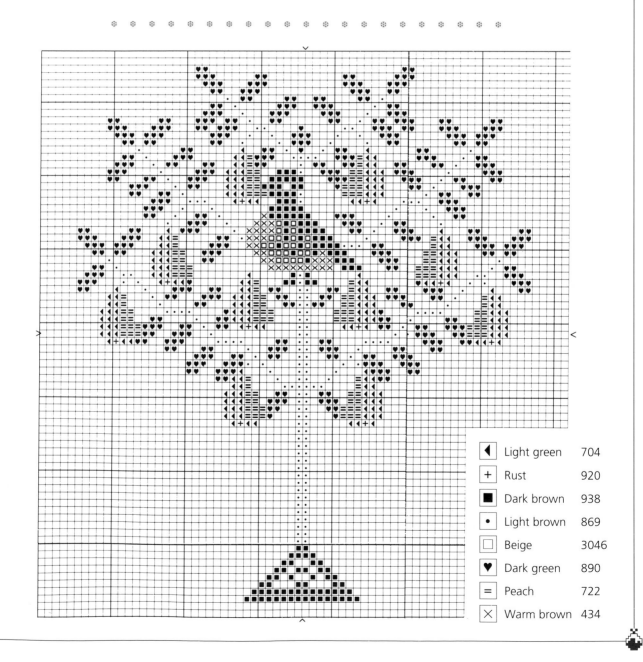

◀	Light green	704
+	Rust	920
■	Dark brown	938
•	Light brown	869
☐	Beige	3046
♥	Dark green	890
=	Peach	722
✕	Warm brown	434

8½ × 7in (215 × 178mm) grey 14-count Yorkshire
  Aida fabric
45in (1,143mm) of ⅝in (16mm) green tartan ribbon
DMC stranded cottons (floss) as shown in the key

1   Find the centre of the design and work outwards from this point following the chart.

2   To frame the design with a similar mount, cut a 3in (76mm) piece from the green tartan ribbon. Fold to form a loop and glue to the top centre back of your chosen frame. Fold the remaining ribbon in half and glue to the top middle edge of the aperture of the cardboard mount, folding the ribbon over at the corners as shown in the photograph. Make a bow, where the ribbons meet at the centre bottom of the aperture, and glue into place to hold flat. Finally, cut the trailing ends of the ribbons into 'fishtails' to neaten.

Alternatives

1   Add the words 'And a partridge in a pear tree' using a back stitch alphabet (see Alternative Alphabets page 118). Position the words just underneath the tree.

2   Work the design on white linen table napkins.

3   Try framing the design with a wreath (as in the Poinsettia design page 28).

FOLK-ART REINDEER

This charming folk-art reindeer, shown here as a card, small hanging and hoop, is a simple Christmas motif adapted from an antique sampler.

For the Card:

Design size: $1\frac{1}{2} \times 1\frac{1}{2}$in (38 × 38mm)
Stitch count: 20 × 20

DMC stranded cottons (floss) as shown in the key
Cream evenweave linen, 28 threads per inch (25mm)
Purchased card (with heart-shaped cut-out)
Glue/impact adhesive

1 Find the centre of the design and following the chart, work in cross stitch using two strands of cotton (floss) over two threads of linen.

2 Glue the embroidery into the card following the manufacturer's instructions.

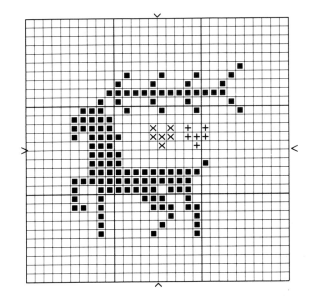

■	Dark brown	3371	+	Dark green	890
✕	Bright red	321			

For the Small Hanging:

Design size: $1\frac{1}{2} \times 1\frac{1}{2}$in (38 × 38mm)
Stitch count: 20 × 20

$5\frac{1}{2} \times 5\frac{1}{2}$in (140 × 140mm) white 14-count Aida fabric
DMC stranded cottons (floss) as shown in the key
Purchased flexi-hoop $3\frac{1}{2}$in (89mm) diameter
7in (178mm) of $\frac{1}{2}$in (13mm) tartan ribbon

1 Follow step 1 as above (but work cross stitch over one block of fabric instead of two threads of linen).

2 Fit the embroidery into the flexi-hoop, making sure that the design is centralised. Trim the excess fabric to within 1in (25mm) of the hoop and make a small turning. Run a gathering thread through the turned edge and gather up the stitches. Secure well.

3 Make a small bow from the tartan ribbon and stitch below the reindeer at the bottom of the hoop so that the stitches do not show.

For the Hoop:

Design size: $2\frac{1}{4} \times 2\frac{1}{2}$in (57 × 64mm)
Stitch count: 28 × 30

5 × 5in (127 × 127mm) unbleached Dublin linen, 25 threads per inch (25mm)
DMC stranded cottons (floss) as shown in the key
4in (102mm) wooden embroidery hoop
7 × 36in (178 × 914mm) dark-green Christmas print fabric
60in (1,524mm) of $\frac{1}{8}$in (3mm) red ribbon
Matching sewing thread

1 Follow step 1 as for the card.

2 When the design is complete, add two 'Noels' from the back stitch alphabet (page 118). Work one in red and one in green and position as shown in the photograph.

3 Repeat step 2 as for the small hanging.

4 Make the hoop frill (see page 124). Sew the red ribbon close to the seam of the frill using a matching sewing thread. Attach the frill to the hoop.

5 Make one small and one large bow from the remaining ribbon and stitch both, with the smaller bow on top of the larger, to the bottom middle of the embroidery (so that it covers the seam in the hoop frill).

6 Finally, to hang the hoop, make a small loop from a piece of left-over ribbon (2in/51mm) and stitch to the centre top at the back of the embroidery.

Alternatives

1 Use the design to decorate table linen. The reindeer could be stitched in a continuous line along the edge of a place-mat or napkin.

2 Replace the hearts with a person's name, stitch on perforated paper and use as a gift tag.

PLUM PUDDING TEDDY

An old-fashioned mob-cap and a large frilly apron, complete with plum pudding and heart motifs, with a holly border, transform this bear into a unique addition for Christmas. The apron front is worked in cross stitch, with additional French knots, using two strands of cotton (floss) over one block of 14-count Aida fabric.

Design size: 4 × 4¾in (102 × 121mm)
Stitch count: 56 × 65

❊ ❊

For the Apron:

5½ × 6in (140 × 152mm) cream 14-count Aida
DMC stranded cottons (floss) as shown in the key
36 × 4in (914 × 102mm) cream cotton fabric (for the apron frill)
46 × 3½in (1,168 × 89mm) cream cotton fabric (for the apron waistband and ties)

1 Find the centre of the design and work outwards from this point following the chart. Work all cross stitches first, then outline the pudding in back stitch using two strands of DMC 3371. Add the French knots using two strands of DMC 321 and positioning them where the heart symbols are shown on the plum pudding.

2 Make a ¼in (6mm) turning on three sides of the 36in (914mm) length of fabric for the frill (one long side and the two short) and either machine or hand stitch, using a matching sewing thread. Gather the remaining long side to fit the curved edge of the apron front (minus ½in/13mm at the top edge where the waistband will be fitted). Adjust the gathers as necessary.

3 Trim the Aida fabric to within ½in (13mm) of the holly border. Make a turning close to the border, pin and tack (baste), and either machine or hand stitch to the frill, leaving a ½in (13mm) gap at the top to attach the waistband.

4 Make a ¼in (6mm) turning on all sides of the remaining length of fabric, fold in half lengthwise and tack (baste), leaving a gap in the middle to insert the apron front. Insert the embroidered apron front into the gap and tack (baste) through all layers. Machine or hand stitch close to the folded edge to complete the ties and the waistband

For the Mob-cap:

16in (406mm) diameter circle of cream cotton fabric
60in (1,524mm) of 1¼in (32mm) cream cotton lace
18in (457mm) cream bias binding
14in (356mm) piece of narrow (¼in/6mm) elastic
Matching sewing thread

1 Using a matching sewing thread zig-zag, or oversew the edge of the fabric circle. Pin and tack (baste) the lace to this edge and machine or hand stitch it in place.

2 Tack (baste) the bias binding 3½in (89mm) in from this edge. Machine or hand stitch, leaving an opening for the elastic.

3 Thread the elastic through the bias binding channel (with a closed safety pin) and join the two ends securely together. Close the opening with tiny stitches.

Alternatives

1 Use the pudding design on gifts or greetings cards.

2 Use the holly border to decorate table linen or the edge of an apron pocket.

Mrs Cratchit entered: flushed, but smiling proudly: with the pudding, like a speckled cannon ball, so hard and firm, blazing in half of half-a-quartern of ignited brandy, and bedight with Christmas holly stuck into the top.

A Christmas Carol CHARLES DICKENS

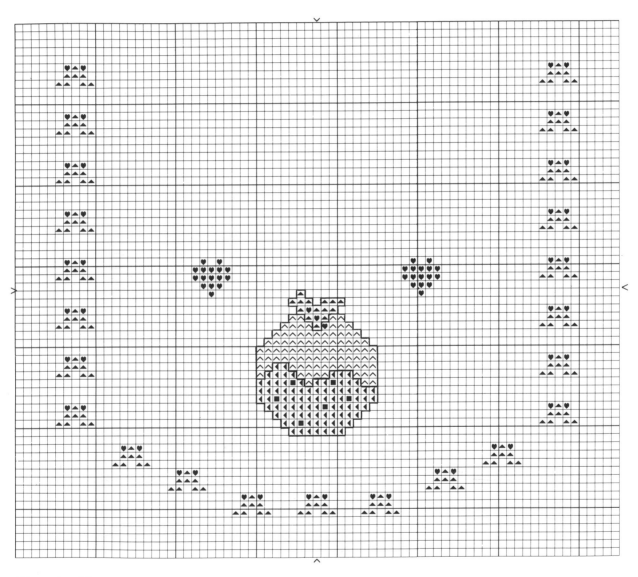

Plum Pudding Teddy

♥	Bright red	321	■	Dark brown	3371
∧	Ecru		◀	Dark beige	610
▲	Holly-green	699		French knots on pudding	321
	Backstitch	3371			

GOLDEN ANGELS

Tiny angels worked in gold thread adorn this small banner and miniature (page 21). Worked in cross stitch over two threads of red linen band, 30 threads per inch (25mm), using DMC gold thread D282, these simple to make, yet highly effective ornaments will add a touch of glitz to your Christmas decor.

❊ ❊ ❊ ❊ ❊ ❊ ❊ ❊ ❊ ❊ ❊ ❊ ❊ ❊ ❊ ❊ ❊ ❊ ❊ ❊

For the Banner:

Design size: 10½ × 2¾in (267 × 70mm)
Stitch count: 135 × 30

22in (559mm) red linen band (with gold edge), 30
    threads per inch (25mm)
DMC gold thread D282
Red sewing thread
Pair of small brass bell-pull hangers

1 Measure 1½in (38mm) from the bottom of the linen band and begin stitching the lower edge of the bottom angel, matching the mid-point on the chart (page 22) to the mid-point of the linen band (widthways).

2 Complete the design in cross stitch following the chart.

3 Make a ½in (13mm) turning at each end of the linen band. Iron on the wrong side and slip stitch these edges together. Slip stitch the sides together, leaving a small gap to insert the brass hangers. (They are split in the middle and therefore easy to insert.)

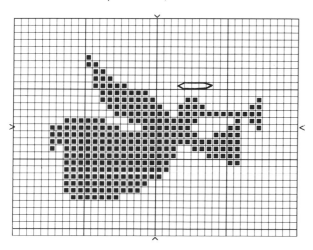

For the Miniature:

Design size: 3 × 2in (76 × 51mm)
Stitch count (of angel): 21 × 30

Small gold-coloured frame
4in (102mm) red linen band, 30 threads per inch
    (25mm)
DMC gold thread D282
Piece of strong card, cut to shape of frame
Glue/impact adhesive

1 Find the centre of the design and work outwards in cross stitch following the chart (page 22).

2 Place the completed embroidery face down, lay the card shape on top and trim the embroidered fabric to an oval shape leaving approximately ¼in (6mm) for overlap. Glue the overlapping edges to the card.

3 Fit the embroidery into the frame.

Alternatives

1 Work the design in brightly coloured space-dyed threads on white linen.

2 Use the motif as a gift tag worked on perforated paper. (Add a name using one of the back stitch alphabets from the Alternative Alphabets (page 118).)

3 Work the design on red or green evenweave linen and frame with a hoop frill in gold-coloured fabric on a 4in (102mm) hoop (see page 124 for making a hoop frill).

GOLDEN ANGELS BOX

Here, the Golden Angel design is used to decorate the lid of a hat box. The design is worked in cross stitch using DMC gold thread D282 on dark-blue 14-count Aida fabric over one block. A box like this would be extremely useful at Christmas for storing all those half written cards and gift tags.

Design size: 4½in (114mm) diameter
Stitch count: 60 × 60

❋ ❋

10 × 10in (254 × 254mm) dark-blue 14-count Aida
  fabric
DMC gold thread D282
One 8in (203mm) hat box kit
27 × 10in (686 × 254mm) dark-blue cotton fabric
8in (203mm) diameter circle of Terylene wadding
  (batting)
52in (1,321mm) of narrow gold ric-rac braid
Glue/impact adhesive
8in (203mm) diameter circle of either black paper or felt
  (for the base)
Matching sewing thread
Straight pins

1 Find the centre of the design and work in cross stitch from this point outwards, following the chart.

2 Make up the hat box and cover the base and lid bands with dark-blue cotton fabric, following the manufacturer's instructions.

3 Lightly glue the Terylene wadding (batting) to the top of the hat box lid. Trim the embroidered fabric to within ¼in (6mm) of the edge of the lid. Turn this edge under and position around the circular top of the box using straight pins.

Oversew to the covered band on the box lid using small stitches.

4 Glue the ric-rac braid to the top and bottom edges of the box lid band.

5 Finally, glue the 8in (203mm) circle of either paper or card to the outside base of the hat box.

Alternatives

1 Cover the box in a Christmas print fabric and use any of the other motifs in the book to decorate the lid.

2 Cover a shoe box in the same way and use a line of angels to decorate (as in the banner).

3 Make your own small box, cover and decorate with just one golden angel. Lined in satin, this would make a wonderful gift box for a special present.

4 Make a much larger hat box and use to store lots of Christmas clutter – ribbon bows, wrapping paper, cards, gift tags – all the things you need to have at hand for the run-up to Christmas.

Golden Angels Box, Banner and Miniature

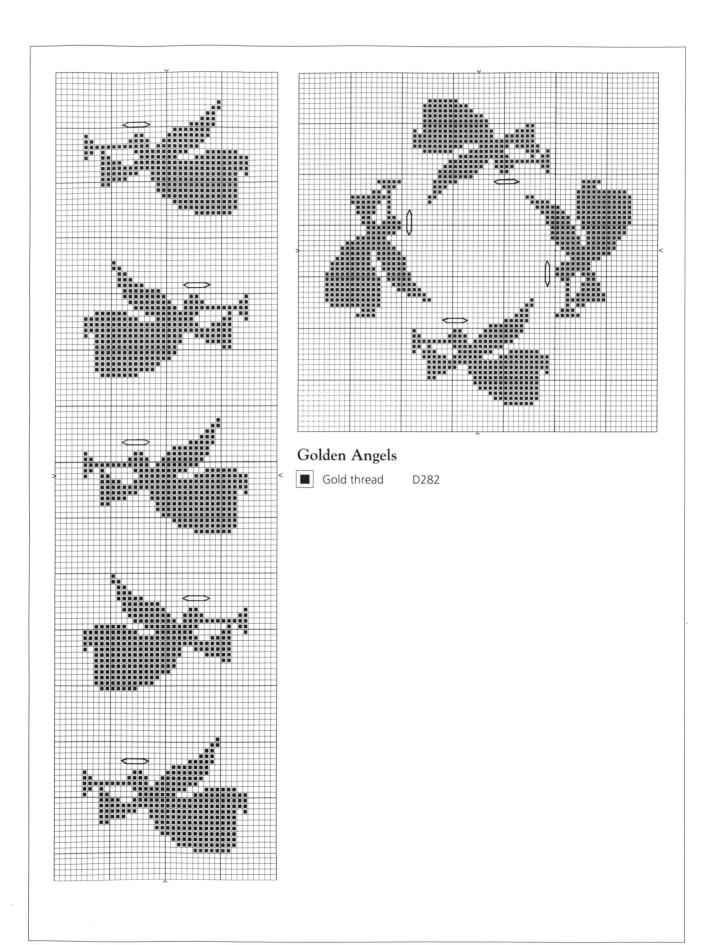

Golden Angels

■ Gold thread   D282

CHRISTMAS SACK

A Christmas sack makes a charming alternative to the Christmas stocking. Why not make one for each of your family? The design (name) is worked in cross stitch using three strands of red variegated cotton (floss) over two threads of linen, then outlined in back stitch using two strands of dark green.

Size (of sack with the top turned over): 11 × 10½in (279 × 267mm) (see also step 2 below)

⁕ ⁕

28½ × 12in (724 × 305mm) tartan fabric
28½ × 12in (724 × 305mm) unbleached Dublin linen
  25 threads per inch (25mm)
28½ × 11in (724 × 279mm) polyester wadding
  (batting)
Stranded cottons (floss) DMC 115 (variegated red) and
  DMC 890 (dark green)
Perlé cotton (5) 500 dark green (for gathering top of sack)
Sewing thread to match the linen and the tartan

1 Begin by measuring 10in (254mm) down from the top of the linen. Mark this line with a row of tacking (basting) stitches.

2 Work out your chosen name in pencil on graph paper. This size of sack will accommodate a name of up to nine letters. (If a longer name is required, simply make your sack a little wider.) Count the number of squares in your chosen name and find the mid-point.

3 Fold your linen in half lightly on the row of tacking (basting) and match this point to the mid-point of your name. Begin stitching here. This will ensure that the name fits the space evenly.

4 Work the lettering as described above, outlining the letters with two strands of dark green DMC 890.

5 When this is complete, fold the linen in half, right sides together. Pin, tack (baste) and either machine or hand stitch the two side seams. Finish seams by oversewing by hand or zig-zagging on the sewing machine. Turn inside out, so that the embroidered name is showing on the outside.

6 Fold the tartan fabric in half with right sides together and repeat the last stage but do not turn inside out.

7 Fold the wadding (batting) in half and oversew the edges together.

8 Assemble the sack by first inserting the wadding (batting) 'bag' inside the linen sack. Attach to the side seams with a few stitches. Next insert the tartan lining. Make ½in (13mm) turnings at the top edge of the linen and the tartan and tack (baste) these edges together (slightly overlapping the tartan). Slip stitch the edges together so that the stitches do not show.

9 Measure down 4in (102mm) from this edge and using four combined lengths 30in (762mm) long of DMC 500 dark green perlé cotton (5), make ½in (13mm) running stitches through the linen, beginning and ending 3in (76mm) in from the right-hand side (front facing). Draw up the running stitches slightly and tie in a knot. Trim the threads to neaten and tie a knot approximately ½in (13mm) from the ends.

10 Turn over the top edge to show the tartan lining.

Alternatives

1 Enlarge the sack and increase the size of the name by working a square of four cross stitches to represent each symbol instead of one. (This will double the size of the name.)

2 Work a family name on a large sack, eg *The Johnsons*.

3 For those with Scottish ancestry, what could be nicer than to choose their own particular tartan to line the sack? Their name could then be worked in colours to match.

4 Make tiny sacks with just one initial for use as tree decorations.

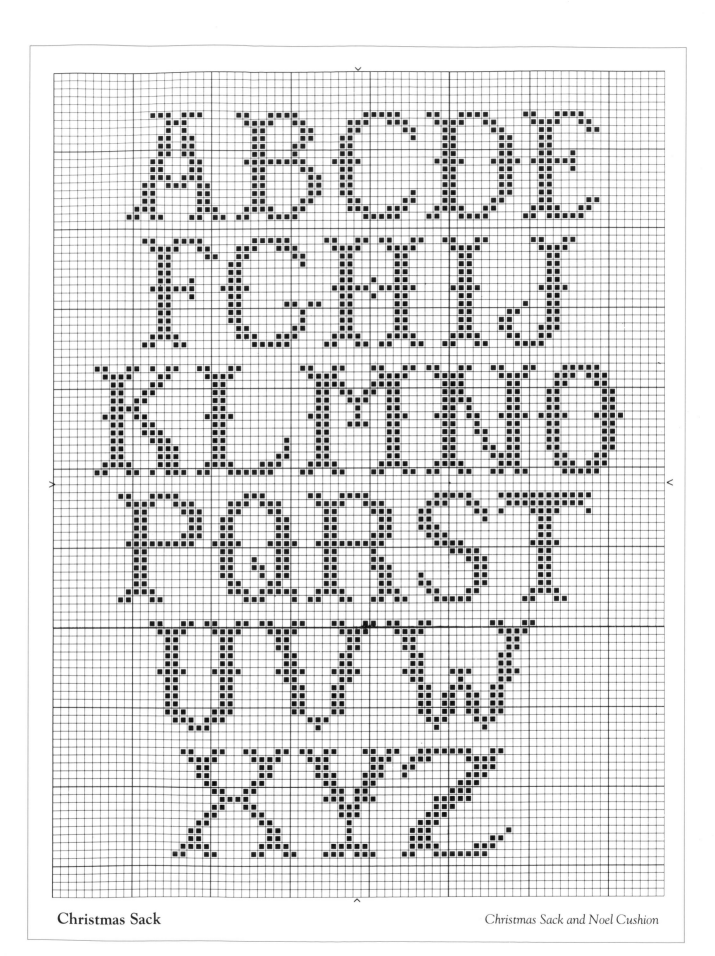

Christmas Sack

Christmas Sack and Noel Cushion

NOEL CUSHION

A red linen band and a beautiful Christmas fabric frill surround this cross stitch design which has been made up as a cushion. Use three strands of embroidery cotton (floss) over two threads of linen.

Design size: $4\frac{1}{2} \times 5$in (114×127mm)
Stitch count: 56×63

❀ ❀

9×9in (229×229mm) white Dublin linen, 25 threads per inch (25mm)
Stranded cottons (floss) as shown in the key
40in (1,016mm) red linen band edged with green 30 threads per inch (25mm)
90×8in ($2,286 \times 203$mm) dark green Christmas print fabric
9×9in (229×229mm) contrasting Christmas print fabric (for backing the cushion)
Matching sewing thread. Polyester fibre filling

1 Find the centre of the design and work outwards from this point, following the chart.

2 Cut the linen band into four 10in (254mm) lengths. Pin and tack (baste) the side pieces $\frac{1}{4}$in (6mm) away from the embroidery. (Use the thread line of the linen as a guide for accuracy.) Machine or hand stitch in a matching thread close to the edge. Lay the top and bottom pieces on the embroidered fabric in the same way, overlapping the linen band at the corners as shown in the photograph. Machine or hand stitch as before.

3 To make the fabric frill you will need to join enough strips of 8in (203mm) fabric to make the required length. Join all the strips together to form one continuous piece. Alternatively, you may have an extremely long piece of fabric (ie cut along the selvedge).

4 When this is done, fold the fabric in half lengthways with the wrong side facing. Tack (baste) rough edges together. Gather along this edge either by machine or hand, then pin and tack (baste) this gathered edge with right sides facing to the embroidered fabric edged with the linen band, easing the gathers as you go.

5 Making sure that the edge of the frill is pointing toward the centre of the work (it is a good idea to tack (baste) this edge down as it is so full), place the piece of contrasting Christmas fabric right side facing on top of the work, matching the edges together. Pin, tack (baste) and then machine through all layers $\frac{1}{2}$in (13mm) from the edge, leaving a 3in (76mm) opening for turning. Remove tacking (basting).

6 Turn, and after filling with the polyester fibre, close the opening with invisible stitches.

Alternatives

1 Attach a loop to the back of the cushion to hang it on a wall or door.

2 Work each of the letters individually and frame using small flexi-hoops for use as tree decorations (or work on perforated paper, cutting around the shape of each letter and hanging with a length of ribbon).

3 Make a banner by working the letters in a line on a narrow piece of linen. Keep repeating the word Noel until the required length is reached. Back with a piece of Christmas fabric.

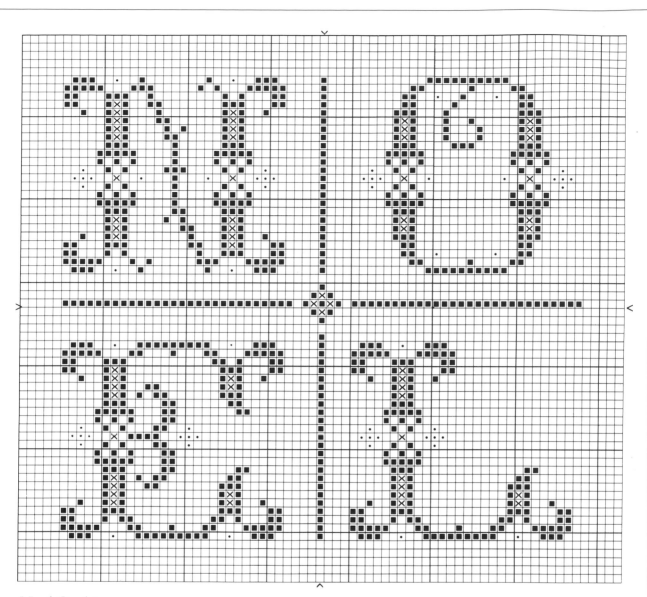

Noel Cushion

✕	Bright red	321
■	Dark green	890
•	Mid green	703

POINSETTIA WREATH AND WOODEN BOWL

The custom of displaying poinsettia plants in the house at Christmas was originally a Mexican idea. The Mexican name for the poinsettia is cuextlaxochitl, meaning 'flower that fades'. Worked in cross stitch over one block of fabric, this charming Poinsettia design will add a wonderful touch to your Christmas decor, and unlike the potted version, can be enjoyed for many years to come.

For the Wreath:

Design size: 3¼ × 3in (82 × 76mm)
Stitch count: 56 × 53

7 × 7in (178 × 178mm) white 18-count Ainring fabric
DMC stranded cottons (floss) as shown in the key
6 × 6in (152 × 152mm) piece of strong card
One 9in (229mm) diameter straw wreath with a 4½in
 (114mm) diameter centre aperture
65in (1,651mm) of ½in (13mm) tartan ribbon
40in (1,016mm) of 2¾in (70mm) dark green taffeta
 ribbon
Glue/impact adhesive
Straight pins

1 Find the centre of the design and following the chart, work outwards with two strands of cotton (floss).

2 Cut a 6in (152mm) diameter circle from the card.

3 Place the embroidery face down on a clean surface. Position the card over the embroidery so that the design is central. Trim the fabric so that ½in (13mm) protrudes from around the edges of the card. Snip the overlapping fabric every inch (25mm) or so to the edge of the card, to allow for turning. Apply adhesive to the overlapping fabric and press on to the card.

4 Wind the narrow tartan ribbon around the straw wreath as shown in the picture and secure at the back with a straight pin. Position the card-covered mount at the back of the wreath and secure with straight pins.

5 Make a large bow from the green taffeta ribbon and secure this to the bottom middle of the wreath with straight pins.

6 Finally, to hang the wreath, make a small loop from a piece of left-over ribbon (2in/51mm) and secure at the top back of the wreath with straight pins.

For the Wooden Bowl:

Design size: 2⅝ × 2½in (67 × 64mm)
Stitch count: 56 × 53

5 × 5in (127 × 127mm) cream 22-count Hardanger
 fabric
DMC stranded cottons (floss) as shown in the key
Purchased 4in (102mm) wooden bowl (Framecraft)

1 Find the centre of the design and working with one strand of cotton (floss) over one block of fabric complete the design from the chart.

2 When your embroidery is complete, fit it into the lid of the wooden bowl, following the manufacturer's instructions.

Alternatives

1 Use the design to decorate table linen.

2 Fit the embroidered design into a small, round brass frame, add a ribbon for hanging and use as a tree decoration.

3 Use the poinsettia motif as a design for a Christmas card.

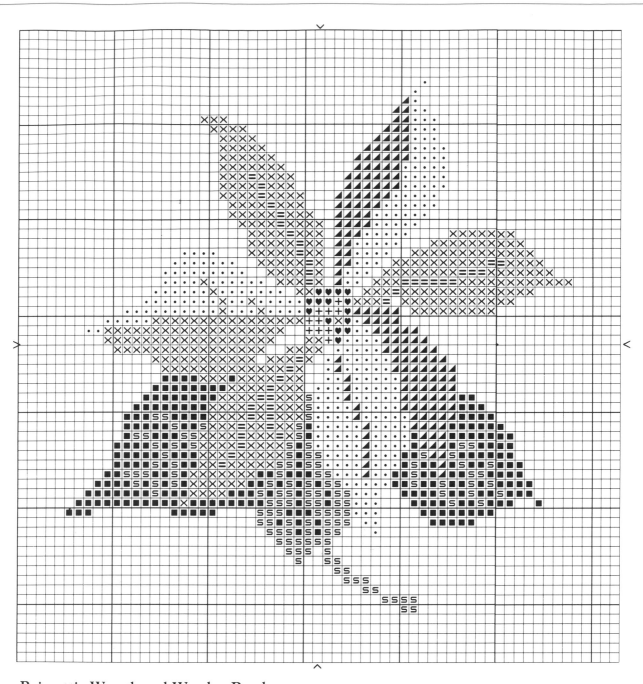

Poinsettia Wreath and Wooden Bowl

✕	Dull red	347	𝖲	Dark sage	730
◢	Bright red	321	■	Dark green	895
•	Orange red	350	♥	Gold	3046
=	Maroon	3685	+	Lemon	744

CHRISTMAS PICTURE

The word Christmas, worked here in cross stitch in zingy colours on black 14-count Aida fabric, is made very decorative by the use of an unusual alphabet. The design has an abstract look which would suit a modern house perfectly. Use two strands of thread throughout.

Design size: 6⅝ × 8⅜in (168 × 213mm)
Stitch count: 91 × 114

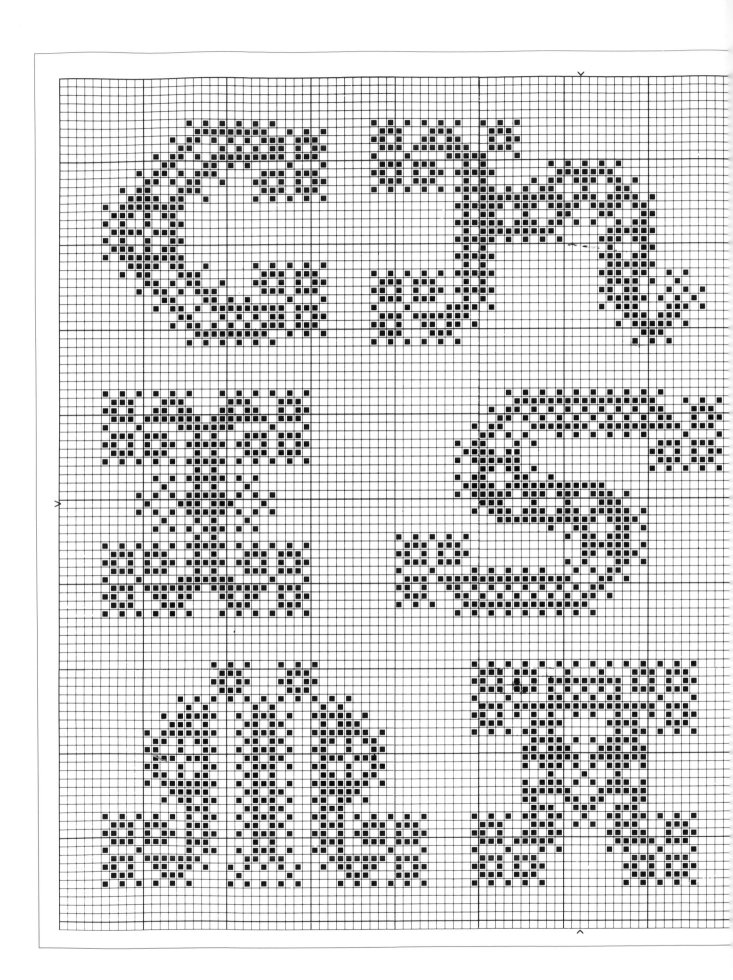

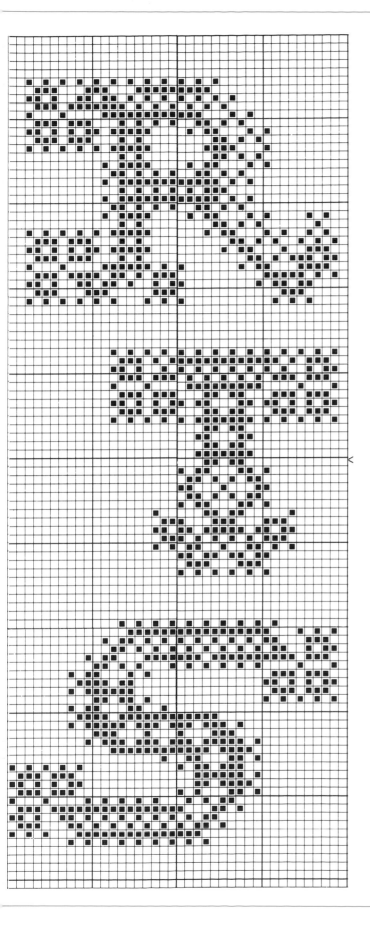

Christmas Picture

Design size: 6⅝ × 8⅜in (168 × 213mm)
Stitch count: 91 × 114

11 × 13in (279 × 330mm) black 14-count Aida fabric
Assorted stranded cottons (floss), flower threads,
 variegated threads, silks, all in zingy
 colours – pinks, purples, turquoise, lilac

Find the centre of the design, match to the centre of the fabric and work outwards from this point using varying lengths of different coloured thread at random.

Alternatives

1 Work each of the letters and frame individually either with purpose-made frames for tree decorations, or make cross-corner frames (see page 43) and paint in colours to match.

2 Work all the letters in a line and use to make a banner.

3 Choose complementary or contrasting colours, for example reds and greens, and work on cream linen for a more traditional design.

4 Use as a panel for a cushion and add a frill in a matching fabric.

ROUND ROBIN

This charming little design featuring robins 'in a round', is very quick and easy to work. Robins featured prominently on Victorian Christmas cards and were said to bear the blood of Christ on their breast. The design is worked in two strands of cotton (floss) over one block of 14-count Aida fabric. Stitches used are cross stitch, back stitch, straight stitch and French knots.

Design size: 3½ × 3½ in (89 × 89mm)
Stitch count: 47 × 47

❋ ❋

7 × 7 in (178 × 178mm) cream 14-count Aida fabric
DMC stranded cottons (floss) as shown in the key

1 It is usually suggested that you find the centre of your fabric and begin working from there, but in this case you should count 24 blocks up from this point and begin working at the top of the robin's head

2 Work the cross, back and straight stitches first and add the French knots last in red DMC 347, positioning them as shown on the chart. Work the robins' feet in half cross stitch in dark brown DMC 938, and all back stitches in dark green DMC 890.

3 Frame as shown or see alternatives opposite.

Alternatives

1 Use the design for a Christmas card. (Choose a purpose-made card with a round aperture.)

2 Make a set of Christmas napkins using this design on linen.

3 Fill a jar with sweets or bath pearls and make a jar lid cover by working the design on a ready-made jar lacy. Or you could make your own by cutting a circle of Aida fabric larger than the circumference of the jar lid. Trim with lace that has eyelet holes. Run a narrow ribbon through the eyelet holes, gather to fit the lid, and tie in a bow.

The North Wind doth blow
And we shall have snow,
And what will the Robin do then,
Poor thing?
He'll sit in a barn
And keep himself warm,
And hide his head under his wing.
Poor thing.

ANON

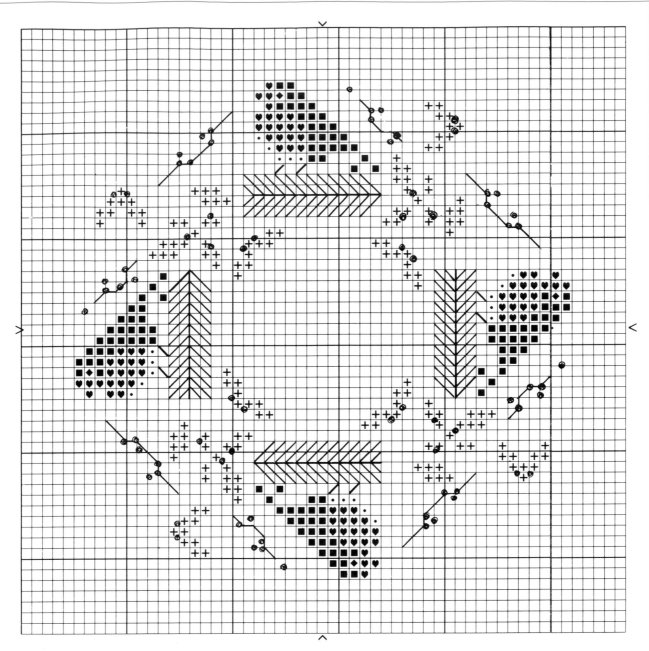

Round Robin

■	Dark brown	938
+	Dark sage	730
♥	Dull red	347
•	Ecru	

♦	Black	310
╱	Back stitch Dark green	890
●	French knots Dull red	347

OLD-FASHIONED SANTA

This charming, old-fashioned Santa in muted colours is based on a wooden carving which originated from the former East Germany. It is worked with two strands of cotton (floss) over one block of fabric.

Design size: 7³/₄ × 4¹/₄in (197 × 108mm)
Stitch count: 143 × 79

11¹/₂ × 8¹/₂in (292 × 215mm) white 18-count Ainring
   fabric
DMC stranded cottons (floss) as shown in the key

Find the centre of the design and work outwards from
this point following the chart.

Alternatives

1   This design would also look wonderful worked
    on unbleached linen over two threads.

2   Try working the design on Cork linen over four
    threads using six strands, for a big, bold Santa on
    a Christmas sack.

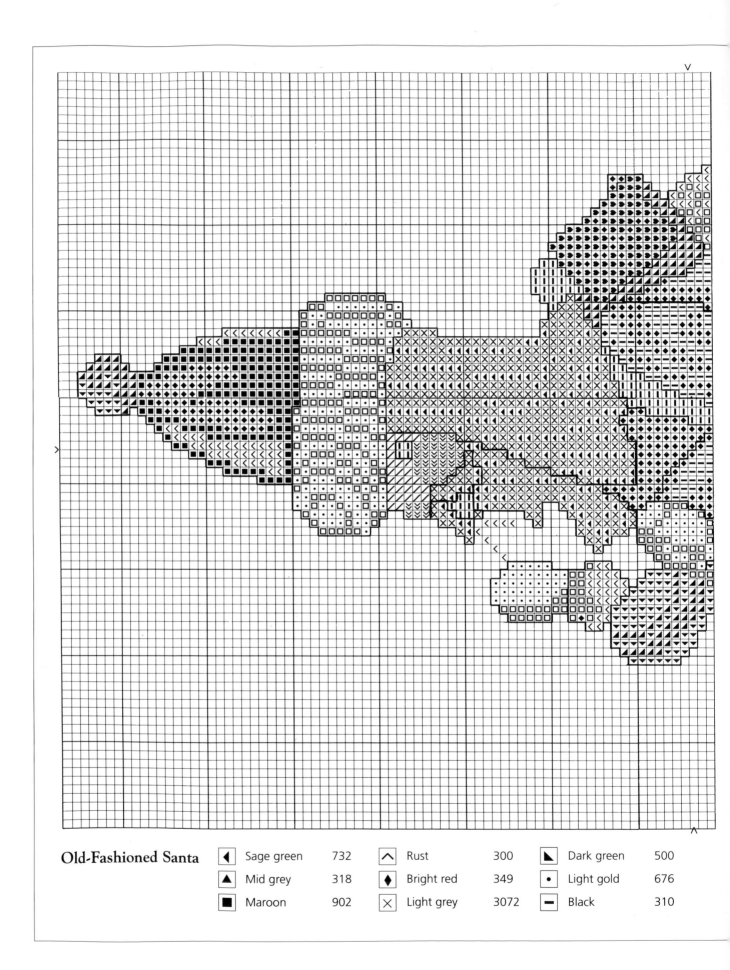

Old-Fashioned Santa

◀	Sage green	732	∧	Rust	300	◣	Dark green	500
▲	Mid grey	318	◆	Bright red	349	•	Light gold	676
■	Maroon	902	✕	Light grey	3072	—	Black	310

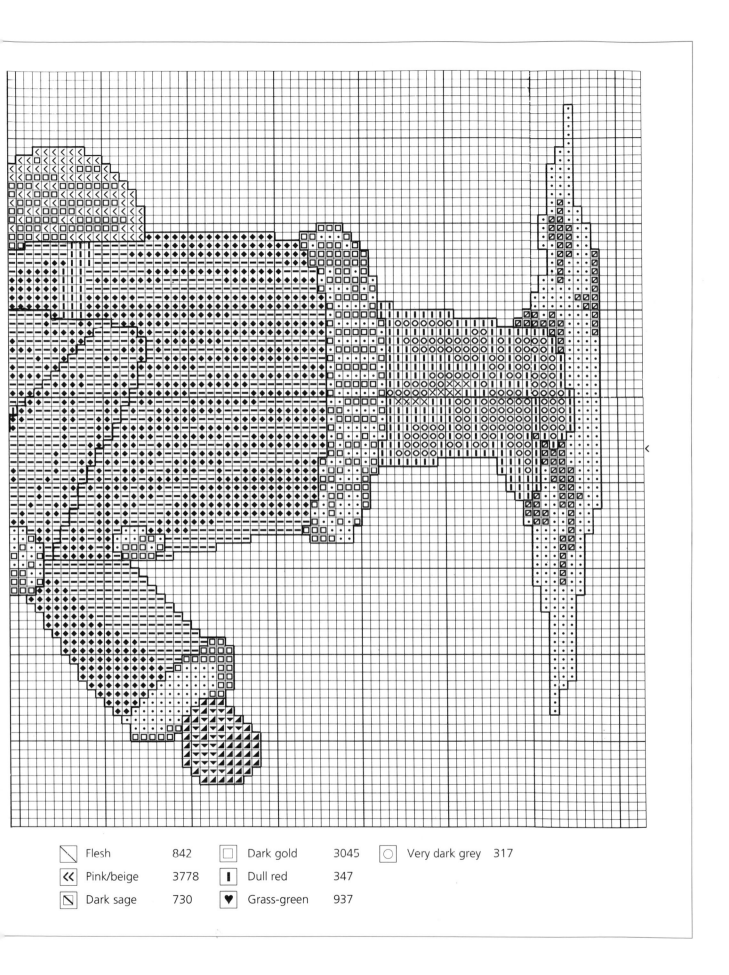

	Flesh	842		Dark gold	3045		Very dark grey	317
	Pink/beige	3778		Dull red	347			
	Dark sage	730		Grass-green	937			

GLORIA IN EXCELSIS DEO

Gloria, Gloria in excelsis Deo.
Gloria, Gloria, sing glory to God on high.

The words of this favourite carol are displayed in an ecclesiastical style, with a sumptuous border worked in back stitch, diagonal satin stitch and cross stitch on cream evenweave linen

Design size: 6 × 5¾in (152 × 146mm)
Stitch count: 88 × 85

❀ ❀

10 × 9in (254 × 229mm) cream Belfast linen, 32
    threads per inch (25mm)
DMC stranded cottons (floss) as shown in the key
DMC gold thread D282

1 Find the centre of the design and work outwards from this point following the chart.

2 The words are worked in cross stitch and back stitch using two strands of cotton (floss) over two threads of linen. The cross stitches are then outlined using *one* thread for emphasis. All back stitch borders and outlines are worked in black DMC 310.

3 The corners of the border are worked in cross stitch using two strands of cotton (floss). The

central cross is worked in diagonal satin stitch using DMC gold thread D282 (do not separate the strands).

4 The scroll border surrounding the words is completed in back stitch using two strands of cotton (floss) over two threads of fabric.

Alternatives

1 Use the design as a bible cover.

2 Work just one section of the border (vertically from corner to corner) on white linen band for use as a bookmark. This would make a wonderful gift.

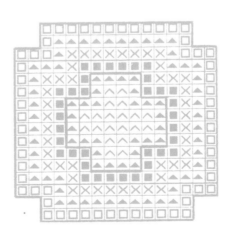

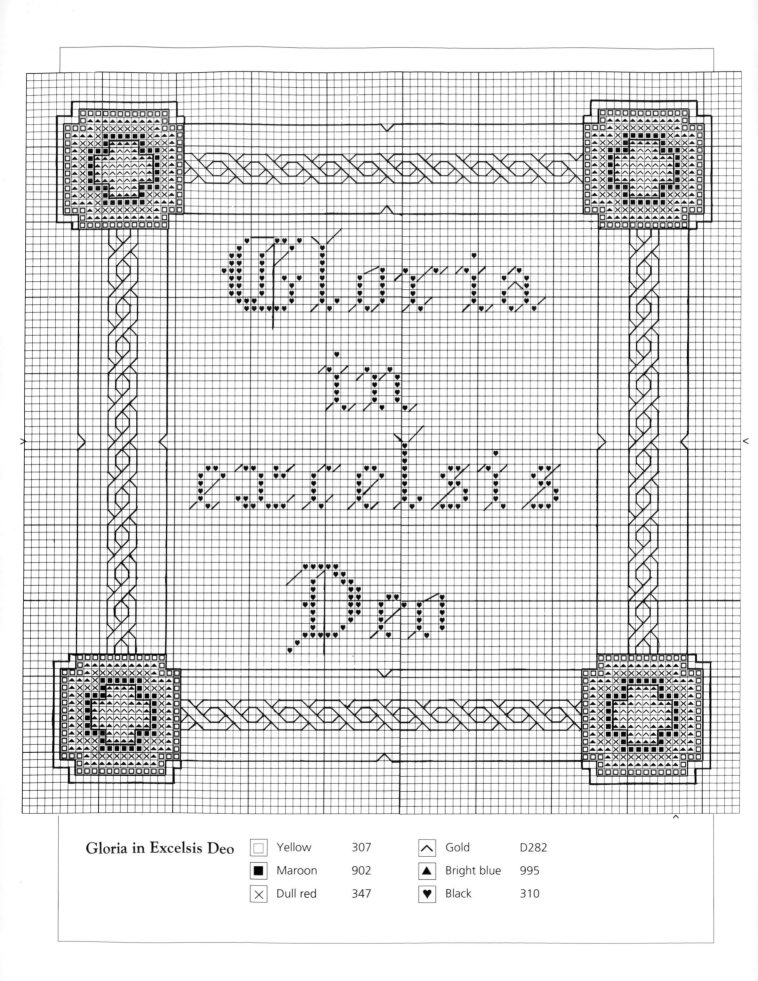

Gloria in Excelsis Deo

☐	Yellow	307	⋀ Gold	D282
■	Maroon	902	▲ Bright blue	995
✕	Dull red	347	♥ Black	310

TREE ORNAMENTS

Wonderfully simple and extremely cheap to make, these unique and effective tree ornaments in their cross-corner frames (overleaf) would be ideal for your own tree, or to sell at a Christmas fair or bazaar. The designs are worked in cross stitch using two strands of embroidery cotton (floss) over two threads of cream or unbleached evenweave linen – cream for the designs in the painted frames and unbleached for the varnished.

❊ ❊ ❊ ❊ ❊ ❊ ❊ ❊ ❊ ❊ ❊ ❊ ❊ ❊ ❊ ❊ ❊ ❊ ❊

Small pieces of cream and unbleached evenweave linen 28 threads per inch (25mm), approximately 4½ × 4½ in (114 × 114mm). The exact size depends on your chosen design
DMC stranded cottons (floss) as shown in the key (pages 46/7)
Cardboard for mounting
Coloured paper for backing
Glue/impact adhesive
Ice-lolly sticks – four for each frame. (You can buy them at craft shops, or do try to recycle your own)
Dark oak varnish
Red and green acrylic paint
Narrow red ribbon ⅛in (3mm) or a colour to match frame (approximately 8in/203mm per frame) or gold thread (for hanging the varnished frames)

1 Choose your design from the charts (pages 46–7), find the centre of the design and match it to the centre of the fabric. Work outwards from this point.

2 When the stitching is complete, cut a piece of card slightly larger than the design. Place your embroidery face down on a clean surface and lay the card on top. Mitre the corners of the overlapping fabric so that they will lie flat when glued down. Trim the fabric to approximately ½in (13mm) bigger than the card all round.

3 Apply adhesive to the overlapping edges of the fabric and also to the outer edge of the card. Leave for one minute and then press the glued sides together, first making sure that the design on the reverse is in the correct position.

4 Lay four ice-lolly sticks just over the edges of your design so that the corners cross as shown in

the picture. When they are correctly aligned, apply a little adhesive to the point on each stick where the corners overlap. Leave for one minute and then glue together.

5 Removing the design from the frame to avoid staining, paint or varnish the frame on both sides and leave to dry. (You may need more than one coat to achieve the desired effect.)

6 Apply a little adhesive to the back of the frame and also to the outside edges of the mounted embroidery where the frame will be fitted. Leave for one minute and glue together.

7 Cut an 8in (203mm) length of ribbon or gold thread and glue to the back of the frame near the top for hanging.

8 Finally, cut a piece of coloured paper slightly smaller than the mounted embroidery and glue to the back of the design.

Alternatives

1 Frame a motif with a mount to make a small picture. This would also make a wonderful stocking filler.

2 Work the alphabet design over one thread in half cross stitch and frame with tiny ice-lolly sticks (or use balsa wood) to make a miniature sampler for a doll's house.

3 Use some of the other small designs in the book and frame in the same way.

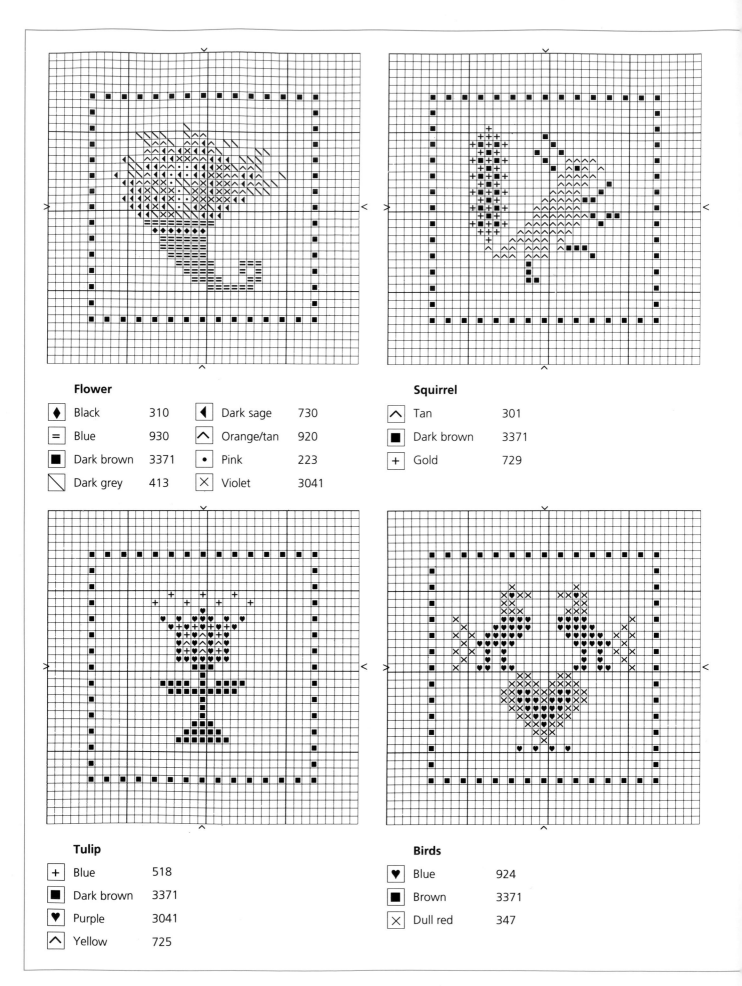

Flower

♦	Black	310	◀	Dark sage	730
=	Blue	930	⋀	Orange/tan	920
■	Dark brown	3371	•	Pink	223
╲	Dark grey	413	✕	Violet	3041

Squirrel

⋀	Tan	301
■	Dark brown	3371
+	Gold	729

Tulip

+	Blue	518
■	Dark brown	3371
♥	Purple	3041
⋀	Yellow	725

Birds

♥	Blue	924
■	Brown	3371
✕	Dull red	347

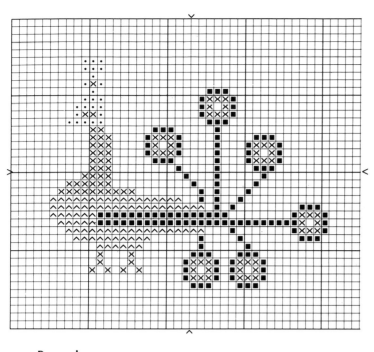

Peacock

■	Maroon	815
•	Ecru	
∧	Pink	223
✕	Dark green	890

Outline peacock's head using one strand of 890

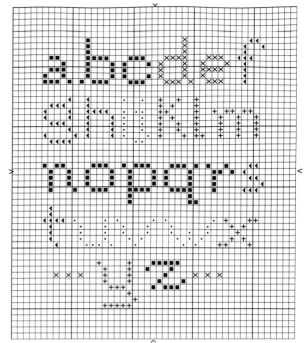

Alphabet Sampler

■	Maroon	815	◀	Orange	971
✕	Dark green	890	•	Yellow	973
+	Gold	832			

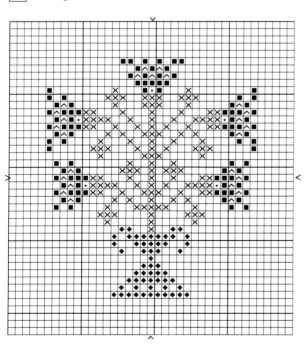

Flower in Pot

•	Yellow	973	✕	Dark sage	730
■	Maroon	815	◆	Dark brown	3371
∧	Pink	223			

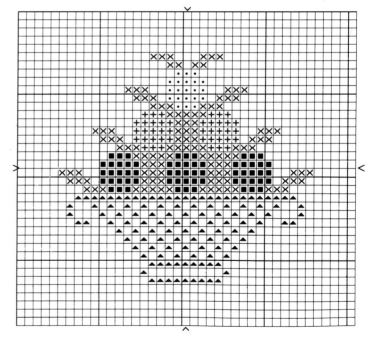

Fruit bowl

•	Yellow	973	■	Maroon	815
+	Orange	971	▲	Dark brown	3371
✕	Dark green	890			

NOEL GUEST TOWEL

This charming little guest towel will add a festive touch to your Christmas decor. The design is worked in cross stitch on a purchased towel with an Aida fabric insert (from needlecraft shops), using DMC stranded cotton (floss) 890 and DMC gold thread D282 over one block of the Aida fabric.

Design size: 9 × 1¾in (229 × 44mm)
Stitch count: 45 × 24

❉ ❉ ❉ ❉ ❉ ❉ ❉ ❉ ❉ ❉ ❉ ❉ ❉ ❉ ❉ ❉ ❉ ❉ ❉ ❉

A purchased guest towel with Aida fabric insert
DMC stranded cottons (floss) as shown in the key

1 Find the centre of the design and match to the centre of the Aida fabric insert.

2 Work the word Noel and the tree from the chart. Using the same base line, work two trees in each side section, (positioning centrally and leaving a gap of seven blocks of fabric between them).

Alternatives

1 Work the word 'Noel' in stranded cotton (floss) with a border of trees embroidered in gold thread for a card.

2 Work the design on linen band and stitch to a plain guest towel.

3 Use the design for Christmas table linen.

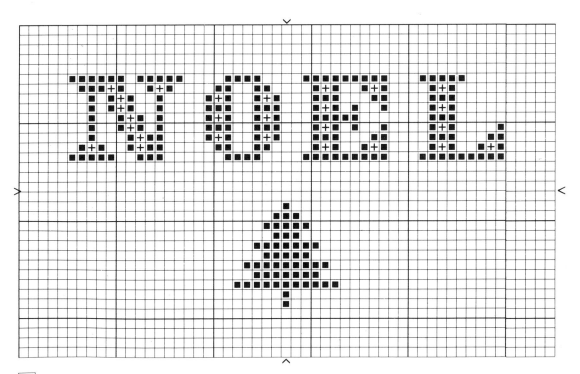

■	Dark green	890
+	Gold thread	D282

COUNTRY CHRISTMAS SAMPLER

This charming Christmas sampler is worked in strong colours in cross stitch, back stitch and French knots, on Rustico fabric to give it a 'country' look.

Design size: 9³/₈in × 7¹/₂in (239 × 190mm)
Stitch count: 126 × 102

❋ ❋ ❋ ❋ ❋ ❋ ❋ ❋ ❋ ❋ ❋ ❋ ❋ ❋ ❋ ❋

13 × 11in (330 × 279mm) 14-count Rustico fabric
DMC stranded cottons (floss) as shown in the key, plus
DMC 926 for outlining

1   Find the centre of the design, match to the centre of the fabric and work outwards from this point following the chart.

2   When all the cross stitching is complete, work the back stitches where indicated. Use one strand of DMC 926 pale blue-grey for outlining the snow flakes. The roof is outlined in DMC 3371 dark brown, the red hearts in DMC 890 dark green. Work the leaded glass effect on the windows of the house using one strand of DMC 3371 dark brown.

3   Finally, using two strands of cotton (floss), work the French knots on the door wreath in DMC 321 red as shown on the chart.

Alternatives

1   Add your family name in place of the lower case alphabet below the house. (Use the larger alphabet and work out in pencil on graph paper.)

2   Use the outer border to decorate table linen.

Country Christmas Sampler and Christmas House

Country Christmas Sampler

■	Navy	823
S	Bright red	321
◆	Dark green	890
=	Warm brown	434
+	Gold brown	676
♥	Dark brown	3371
◇	Yellow	307
•	Ecru	
◀	Bright blue	792
∧	Light sage	733
╱	Bright green	699
╲	Light green	472

CHRISTMAS HOUSE

*A warm glow exudes from the windows of this welcoming little house (page 51).
Worked in cross stitch over two strands of linen, the house motif is part of the
Country Christmas Sampler design (see page 53). A simple border, two tiny bows
and a house-shaped frame transform it into a charming design to
brighten your home at Christmas.*

Design size: 4¼ × 3¾in (108 × 95mm)
Stitch count: 38 × 47

✼ ✼

8 × 6in (203 × 152mm) white Dublin linen, 25 threads
  per inch (25mm)
DMC stranded cottons (floss) as shown in the key
6in (152mm) of ⅛in (3mm) red ribbon
6in (152mm) of ⅛in (3mm) green ribbon
Purchased house-shaped frame
Tacking (basting) thread

1 Measure up 2¾in (70mm) from the bottom edge
of the linen and work a line of tacking (basting)
stitches. This is the base line for the house. Find
the centre point on this line and match it to the
centre square of the base of the house on the
Country Christmas Sampler chart. Begin
stitching here using two strands of cotton (floss).

2 When the house is complete, measure 1⅛in
(28mm) from its base and work a line of tacking
(basting) stitches. This is the base line for
the border.

3 Find the centre point of the heart and holly
border (above the trees and numerals border on
the Country Christmas Sampler). Match it to
the centre point on this line and begin
stitching here.

4 When all the cross stitching is complete,
work the back stitches and French knots as
shown on the chart, again using two strands of
cotton (floss).

5 Make small bows from the red and green ribbon
and attach with small invisible stitches in a
matching thread. Position as shown on the
photograph, if using this type of frame.

6 Mount your embroidery on the card provided (if
using the frame shown) or simply stretch, mount
and frame as required.

Alternatives

1 Add your family name just underneath the
house using one of the alphabets from the
Alternative Alphabets section (page 118–19). If
you wish to use a large alphabet like the one used
on the Christmas Sack (page 24) simply omit
the border.

2 Frame with a double mount of red and green in
an oblong frame with an appropriate saying, for
example, Home is where the heart is or All
hearts come home for Christmas.

GOLDEN TREE IN THE FOREST

This delightful design of repeated tree motifs (overleaf) is worked in green variegated and gold thread on unbleached Edinburgh linen, 36 threads per inch (25mm). The addition of a heavy cord framing the mount and a golden bow add impact to this stunning design. Use two strands of embroidery cotton (floss) over two threads of linen.

Design size: 6 × 7in (152 × 178mm)
Stitch count: 87 × 105

❋ ❋

10 × 11in (254 × 279mm) unbleached Edinburgh
   linen, 36 threads per inch (25mm)
DMC stranded cotton (floss), variegated 122
DMC gold thread D282 (unstranded)
9 × 10in (229 × 254mm) piece of strong card for
   mounting
One dark green and one gold-coloured mount, cut to
   shape
30in (762mm) heavy, dark green cord
Two 12in (305mm) lengths of gold-coloured crochet
   cotton (or several lengths of gold thread)
Glue/impact adhesive

1   Find the centre of the design on the chart
overleaf, match to the centre of the fabric and
work outwards from this point.

2   Lace the completed embroidery on to the piece
of strong card (see page 121) and glue first the
gold-coloured then the dark green cut mounts.

3   Apply a line of adhesive approximately ¼in
(6mm) away from the edge of the dark green
outer mount and leave for one minute until the
adhesive becomes tacky. Press the cord on to the
line of adhesive starting at the mid-point at the
bottom. Trim, so that the ends just meet and
apply a little extra adhesive at this point to
prevent fraying.

4   Make a bow with the two lengths of crochet
cotton and glue to the point where the ends of
the cord meet.

Alternatives

1   Make the design smaller by using fewer of the
tree motifs and make up into a Christmas card.

2   Use the tree motif for small tree ornaments.
They would look wonderful worked on
perforated paper, cut to shape and hung with a
bright ribbon.

3   Have your picture framer make you a tree-shaped
frame.

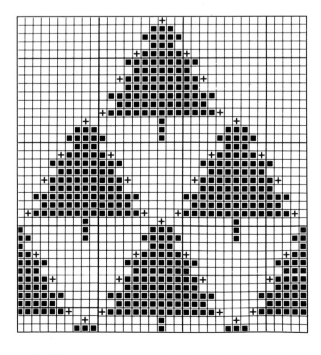

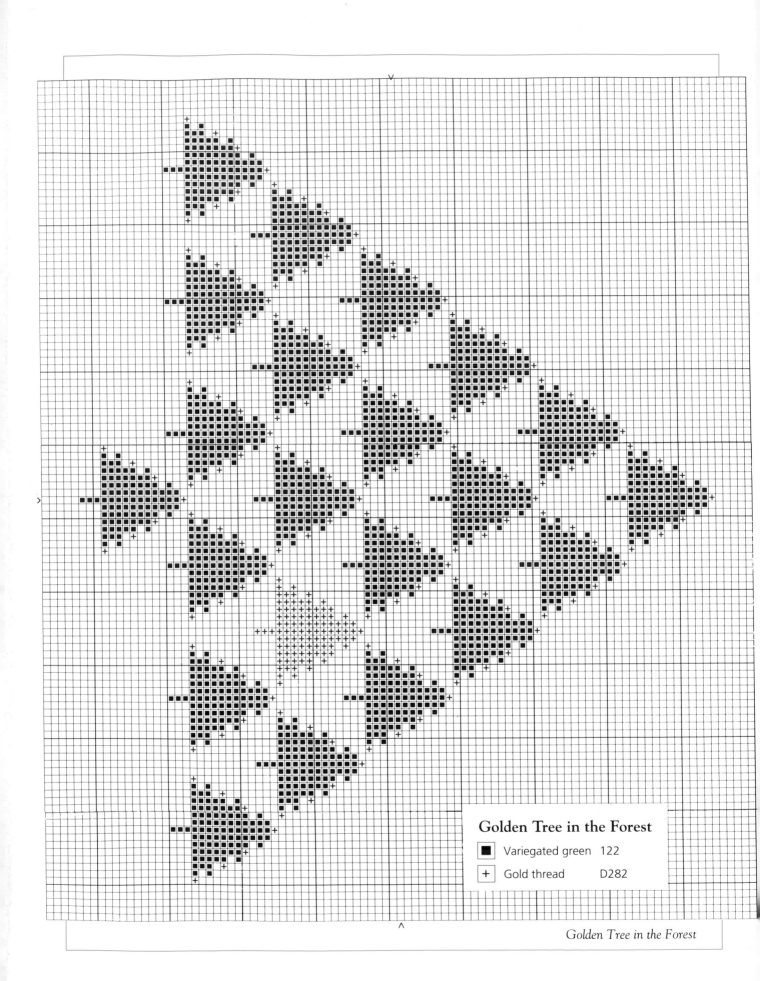

Golden Tree in the Forest

■ Variegated green   122

+ Gold thread   D282

Golden Tree in the Forest

COUNTRY CHRISTMAS KITCHEN

A colourful apron, oven gloves and jam pot cover decorated with country-style motifs, add up to a warm and welcoming country Christmas in the kitchen. The designs are all worked in stranded cotton (floss).

For the Apron:

Design size: 5½ × 1⅛in (140 × 28mm)
Stitch count: 81 × 15

Purchased apron in red cotton fabric (or make your own)
12in (305mm) piece of 2¾in (70mm) linen band with pale green edging, 30 threads per inch (25mm)
DMC stranded cottons (floss) as shown in the key
Matching sewing thread (for stitching the linen band to the apron)

1 Find the centre of the design (from the horizontal chart overleaf) and match to the centre of the linen band. Work in cross stitch using two strands of cotton (floss) over two threads of linen.

2 Trim the embroidered linen band to the shape of the apron top leaving an extra ¼in (6mm) for turnings. Turn in the short ends and making sure that the design is centralised, pin, tack (baste) and either machine or hand stitch close to the edge.

For the Oven Gloves:

Design size: 5½in × 1⅛in (140 × 28mm)
Stitch count: 81 × 15

Purchased oven gloves
Two 7½in (190mm) pieces of 2¾in (70mm) linen band with pale green edging, 30 threads per inch (25mm)
DMC stranded cottons (floss) as shown in the key
Matching sewing thread (for stitching the linen band to the oven gloves)

1 Follow step 1 as for the apron.

2 Follow step 2, trimming the linen bands to the width of the oven gloves plus ¼in (6mm) turnings.

For the Jam Pot Cover:

Design size: 1¾ × 1⅝in (44 × 41mm)
Stitch count: 32 × 30

Purchased jar lacy
DMC stranded cottons (floss) as shown in the key
18in (457mm) of ⅛in (3mm) red ribbon

1 Find the centre of the design (from the square chart overleaf), match to the centre of the jar lacy and work in cross stitch using two strands of cotton (floss) over one block of fabric.

2 Thread the ribbon through the holes in the jar lacy and fit to the top of the jam pot by pulling the ribbons tight and tying in a bow.

Alternatives

1 Work the design from the square chart and frame in a small wooden frame for a country kitchen.

2 Work the design in white on red linen band and stitch to the hem of a white apron, or to edge a tea towel.

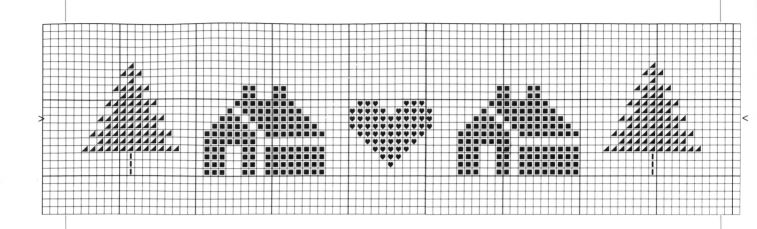

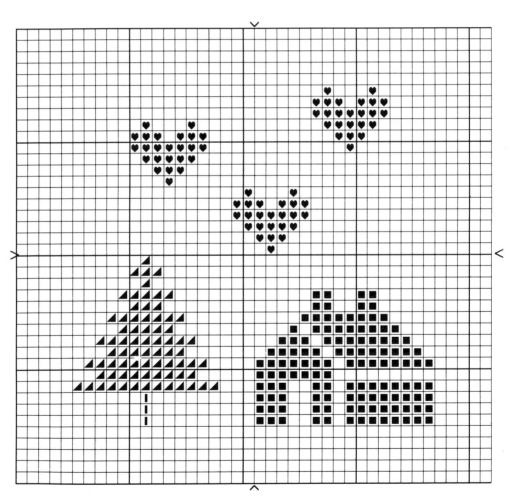

Country Christmas Kitchen

♥	Bright red	321
■	Dark brown	3371
◢	Dark green	890
I	Light brown	434

MERRY CHRISTMAS AROUND THE WORLD

The greeting 'Merry Christmas' is shown in many languages to delightful effect in this charming hoop design (overleaf). The design is worked in cross stitch and back stitch on white Dublin linen. Use one strand of DMC perlé cotton (5) throughout.

Design size: 14 × 16½in (356 × 419mm)
Stitch count: 177 × 203

❋ ❋

22 × 22in (559 × 559mm) white Dublin linen, 25 threads per inch (25mm)
DMC perlé cottons (5), as shown in the key (page 65)
DMC cotton perlé (5) bright green 909, grey/green 935 and variegated red 115
One 18in (457mm) diameter quilting hoop
20 × 20in (508 × 508mm) white cotton fabric (for backing)
Matching sewing thread

For the Plait:

88 × 4½in (2,235 × 114mm) red cotton chintz fabric
88 × 4½in (2,235 × 114mm) green cotton chintz fabric
88 × 4½in (2,235 × 114mm) Christmas-patterned fabric
Three 88 × 2in (2,235 × 51mm) lengths polyester wadding (batting)

For the Bow:

Two 10½in × 5½in (267 × 140mm) pieces red cotton chintz fabric
5½ × 3in (140 × 76mm) green cotton chintz fabric
Four 13 × 4½in (330 × 114mm) pieces red chintz fabric
10 × 5in (254 × 127mm) polyester filling
Small piece of ribbon or fabric 5 × 1in (127 × 25mm) for hanging loop

1 Find the centre of the design on the chart (pages 64–5), match to the centre of the fabric and work outwards from this point. *Felices Pascuas* is worked in backstitch DMC cotton perlé(5) bright green 909; *Noeliniz kutlu olsun* in grey-green 935 and *Nollaig faoi shéan agus faoi shonas duit* in variegated red 115.

2 When the embroidery is complete, centre the design in the hoop. Trim away the excess linen to within 1in (25mm) from the edge of the hoop and oversew to prevent fraying.

3 Cut a 19in (483mm) circle from the white cotton fabric, make a ½in (13mm) turning and tack (baste). Slip stitch the circle, with wrong sides facing, to the back of the hoop to cover the raw edges of the embroidered fabric.

4 Lay an 88 × 4½in (2,235 × 114mm) strip of the red chintz fabric on a flat surface with the wrong side facing. (If necessary, join strips to achieve this length.) Place a strip of wadding (batting) centrally on the strip of fabric. Fold the bottom edge of the chintz fabric up to the middle of the wadding (batting) and tack (baste) through both layers. Make a ¼in (6mm) turning on the top edge of the fabric and fold down on to the tacking (basting). Tack (baste) through all layers to hold in place and then slip stitch the seam. Remove tacking (basting).

5 Repeat this process for the two remaining lengths of green and Christmas-patterned fabric.

6 Tack (baste) all three lengths together at one end. Anchor this end to a door handle, or ask a friend to hold it for you. Plait the three lengths together evenly. Secure the ends by tacking (basting) together.

7 Beginning at the bottom of the hoop in the middle, pin around the edge so that approximately ½in (13mm) overlaps the embroidered fabric. Slip stitch into place, trim the plait to size, and join the edges together with small stitches.

8 For the bow, start with the two 10½ × 5½in (267 × 140mm) pieces of red cotton chintz. With right sides together pin, tack (baste) and either machine or hand stitch the 'bow' pieces together, approximately ¼in (6mm) from the edge, leaving a small gap for turning. Turn, and after stuffing loosely with the polyester filling, close the gap with small stitches.

9 Fold the piece of green chintz long sides to middle and wrap around the centre of the padded tube. Adjust size to fit and oversew the ends together.

10 Using the four red chintz fabric pieces for the trailing 'tails' of the bow, place two pieces right sides together. Measure 4in (102mm) along one of the long edges. Draw a line in pencil from this point to the nearest opposite corner.

Cut along this line to form the points for the ribbon 'tails'. Pin, tack (baste) and either machine or hand stitch the pieces together, leaving a small gap for turning. Turn and close the gap with small stitches. Repeat for the other ribbon 'tail'.

11 Stitch these ribbon 'tails' in place at the bottom middle of the hoop. Secure firmly. Place the padded bow over the stitches and slip stitch into place so that the stitches do not show.

12 Finally, to hang the hoop, make a loop from a small piece of fabric or ribbon and stitch to the centre top at the back of the embroidery.

Alternatives

1 Work the greetings individually or choose one or two of them for use as Christmas cards.

2 Rearrange the greetings into a long oblong shape and make up as a Christmas banner.

MERRY CHRISTMAS AROUND THE WORLD

Felices Pascuas	*Spanish*
Noeliniz kutlu olsun	*Turkish*
Nadolig Llawen	*Welsh*
Gledelig Jul	*Norwegian*
Buon Natale	*Italian*
Nollaig faoi	*Irish*
shéan agus	
faoi shonas	
duit	
Vrolijk Kerstmis	*Dutch*
Joyeux Noel	*French*
Fröhliche Weihnachten	*German*

Merry Christmas Around the World

■	Red	815
◢	Grey/green	935
+	Light sage	581
♦	Bright red	321
♥	Dark green	895
−	Green	936

SATIN STITCH SANTAS

These delightful Santas with their overlarge moustaches and huge hats are worked on plastic canvas with wool (woollen yarn). Their moustaches are made with wool roving. Why not work one in each colour-way and display them side by side? Children in particular will love their comic look.

Size: approximately 8in (203mm) high

✳ ✳

2 pieces of 7-point plastic canvas 9¼ × 7in (235 × 178mm)
Two 500g (16oz) balls double knitting wool (use for knitting and satin stitch) – one red and one dark green
DMC Laine Colbert Tapisserie wool in ecru, noir, 7950 pink/beige, 7171 flesh
One pack of wool roving (or use angel hair) for the moustache

1 Find the centre of the design and following the chart, thread your needle with two lengths of wool (woollen yarn), working in vertical satin stitch over two threads of plastic canvas.

2 To make the nose, thread your needle with one length of pink/beige wool (woollen yarn) and, positioning as shown on the chart, work a large French knot (wind the wool several times around the needle).

3 Take an 11in (279mm) piece of wool roving and pull the ends until they are teased into a moustache shape. Fold in half and oversew at the mid-point to the canvas, just below the nose, using a matching thread.

4 Form the embroidered plastic canvas into a tube and oversew the edges together at the back.

5 To complete the hat, use 2¾mm (USA size 2) knitting needles and cast on 60sts.
 Work in k1, p1 rib for 2½in (64mm)
 Change to 3¼mm (USA size 3) needles
1st row: inc knit-wise into every 5th st
2nd row: purl
3rd row: inc knit-wise into every 5th st
Continue in stocking st, until work measures 6in (152mm) finishing on a purl row

1st row: knit 11, knit two together. Repeat to the end of the row
2nd row: purl
3rd row: knit 10, knit two together. Repeat to the end of the row
4th row: purl
Continue to decrease in this way, ie 4th row knit 9; 5th row knit 8 until 38 sts remain.
Continue working without further decreasing until work measures 12in (305mm).
 k: knit
 p: purl
 inc: increase
 st: stitch
 sts: stitches

6 Break off yarn leaving a long length. Thread through the remaining sts, then pull up tightly and secure but do not break off the length. Place right sides together, pin and back stitch using the long length that is still attached. Oversew the rib section. Turn and fold back the rib of the hat.

7 Make a 2in (51mm) long tassel (see Finishing Techniques) and sew firmly to the end of the hat.

8 Finally, fit the hat on to your Santa and secure with a few small stitches at the sides of the head.

Alternatives

1 Scale down the size of the Santas, make the hats from felt, add a loop made from ribbon or card and use as tree decorations.

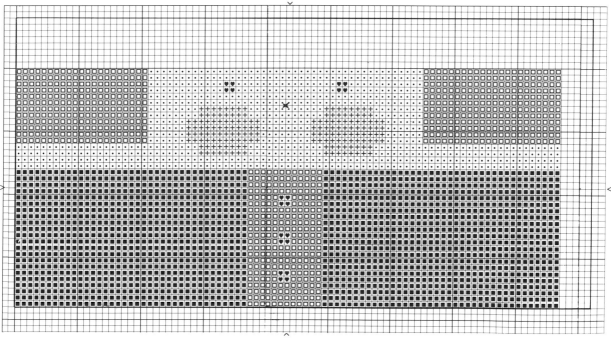

Satin Stitch Santas

■	Red (or green)	□	Ecru
♥	Noir	+	Pink 7950

● Flesh 7171

✕ position for nose

STENCIL SANTA

This Stencil Santa has a delightfully old-fashioned look and is worked in cross stitch and back stitch using two strands of embroidery cotton (floss) on perforated paper.

Design size: 6½in × 5in (165 × 127mm)
Stitch count: 91 × 69

❀ ❀ ❀ ❀ ❀ ❀ ❀ ❀ ❀ ❀

8 × 6½in (203 × 165mm) white 14-count perforated paper
DMC stranded cottons (floss) as shown in the key

1 Find the centre of the design, match to the centre of the paper and work outwards from this point.

2 When the design is complete, cut carefully around the edge about ⅛in (3mm) away from the design using sharp scissors and taking care not to cut into any of the stitching.

3 Frame as shown in the picture or see alternatives below.

Alternatives

1 When cutting out leave extra paper in a small rounded shape at the top of Santa's head. Punch a hole through this extra 'bump' and thread a narrow ribbon through. The design can then be hung on a tree.

2 Work the design on linen or Aida fabric and frame, or use as a panel for a cushion.

3 Use the design on a child's Christmas stocking or sack.

4 Work the design on perforated paper. Mount on stiff paper and make up as a Christmas card.

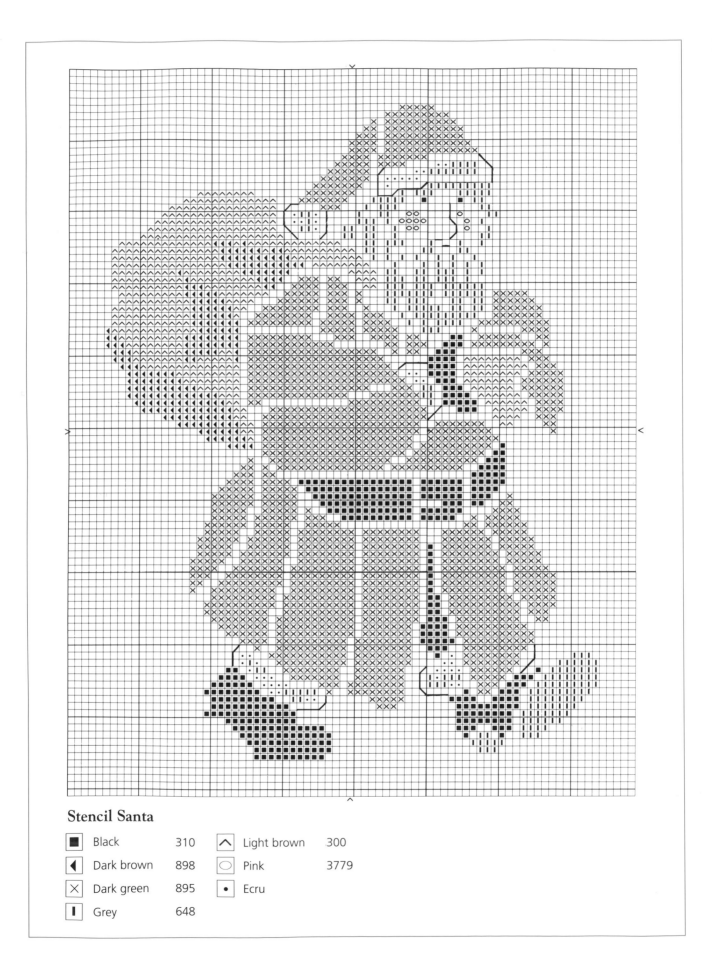

Stencil Santa

■	Black	310	∧	Light brown	300
◀	Dark brown	898	○	Pink	3779
✕	Dark green	895	•	Ecru	
I	Grey	648			

SILENT NIGHT CARD

A church at night is the theme for this striking design (see overleaf) worked in shades of purple and blue on a white evenweave fabric. The design is simplicity itself and uses scraps of left-over thread. The technique used is known as voiding, where the design itself is left unworked and the background is filled in with cross stitch.

Design size (of aperture of card): 5 × 3¼in (127 × 82mm). This of course will vary according to the aperture of your chosen card.

❊ ❊

7 × 5½in (178 × 140mm) white evenweave linen, 28
   threads per inch (25mm)
Assorted stranded cottons (floss), flower threads, silks, in
   shades of purple and blue
Purchased card (or make your own)
Glue/impact adhesive
Tacking (basting) thread

1 Outline the design in tacking (basting) thread,
following the chart and positioning in the centre
of the fabric.

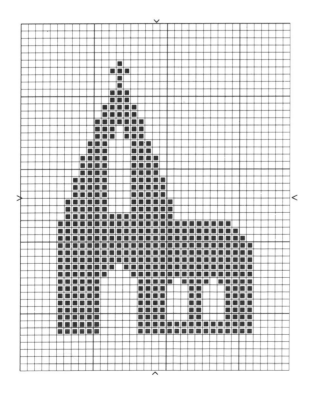

2 Using two strands of embroidery cotton (floss)
over two threads of fabric, fill in the background
in cross stitch leaving the church motif itself
unworked. Use varying lengths of different
threads in a random fashion. Start with pale
shades at the top of the design, introducing
darker shades nearer the bottom. Try also
blending threads by threading your needle with
two different colours at the same time. This
technique is much easier than it looks and once
mastered can be used to great effect in a number
of exciting ways.

3 When the background is completely filled in, ie,
enough to fill the aperture of your chosen card,
remove the tacking (basting) threads.

4 Fit the design into the card following the
instructions given in Finishing Techniques.

Alternatives

1 Frame as a picture with or without a mount.

2 Use a small silver frame for a very special tree
decoration.

3 Leave a block of fabric unworked underneath the
design and, using one of the alphabets given in
Alternative Alphabets, work the name of your
church, ie St Luke's. (For a Christmas wedding,
you could also add the names of the bride and
groom and the date.)

BAROQUE TREE ORNAMENTS

Stylish and original, these elegant ornaments are worked in Decor no 6, a shiny rayon thread, and crewel wool in cross stitch over two threads of canvas.

Design size (of maroon ornament): $2\frac{7}{8} \times 1\frac{3}{4}$in ($73 \times 44$mm)(of blue ornament): $2\frac{3}{8} \times 2\frac{1}{8}$in ($61$mm $\times 54$mm)
Stitch count (of maroon ornament): 31×19(of blue ornament): 29×23

Silent Night Card and Baroque Tree Ornaments

4½ × 4in (114 × 102mm) white 22-count petit point
   canvas
Madeira Decor no 6 1558 rayon thread in rust (or
   substitute DMC gold thread D282)
DMC crewel wool (Medici) maroon 8110 and/or blue
   8206
4½ × 4in (114 × 102mm) cotton velvet fabric in
   maroon and/or blue, for backing
Matching sewing thread
Polyester filling

1 Find the centre of the design, match to the
centre of the canvas and work outwards from this
point following the chart. Work the motif in rust
(or DMC gold thread D282) and the background
in either the maroon or blue crewel wool.

2 Place the completed embroidery and the velvet
backing right sides together. Pin, tack (baste)
and either machine or hand stitch together,
about ¼in (6mm) away from the embroidery,
leaving a gap for turning. Trim excess fabric and
canvas to within ¼in (6mm) of the seam.
Remove the tacking (basting) stitches.

3 Turn, and after filling with polyester fibre, close
the opening with tiny stitches.

4 Make the cord and the long tassel (see
Finishing Techniques) from either the Decor
thread or the alternative DMC gold thread.
Beginning at the bottom middle, slip stitch the
cord to the edge using small stitches in a
matching thread. Make a long hanging loop at
the centre top, securing firmly at this point.
Continue slip stitching the remaining side and
secure the ends firmly by overstitching. Stitch
the tassel to cover the join, then secure firmly.

Alternatives

1 Try working contrasting coloured backgrounds
eg emerald green, crimson or purple.

2 Use the design for the lid of a trinket pot.

3 Frame using purchased brass tree ornament
frames and hang with coloured ribbon.

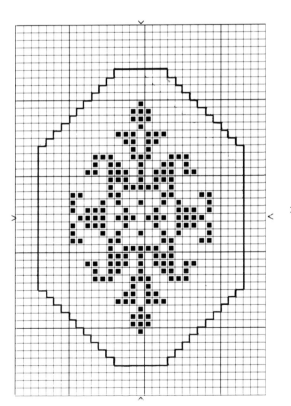

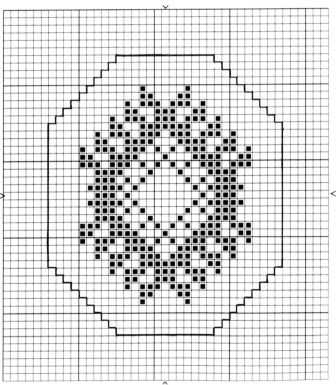

HOLLY STOCKING

This bright and cheerful traditional Christmas stocking, complete with a child's name and applied red ribbon stripes, is sure to please. It is worked in cross stitch with DMC stranded cotton (floss) over two blocks of white Hardanger fabric with an additional linen band. Lined in white cotton and backed with red chintz, it is a perfect addition to the Christmas fireplace.

Size of stocking: 18in (457mm) length
Stitch count (of holly motif): 24 × 21

DMC stranded cottons (floss) as shown in the key
  (page 78)
21 × 17in (533 × 432mm) white 22-count Hardanger
  fabric
40in (1,016mm) of narrow ⅛in (3mm) red satin ribbon
8½in (215mm) white linen band, 28 threads per inch
  (25mm)
21 × 34in (533 × 864mm) white cotton fabric for lining
8½ × 1in (215 × 25mm) length of red chintz
21 × 17in (533 × 432mm) red cotton chintz fabric
16½ × 1in (419 × 25mm) length of red chintz
7 × 2½in (178 × 64mm) length of red chintz
50in (1,270mm) green edging cord
Matching sewing thread

1 Following the shape of the stocking as it is marked on the chart (pages 78–9), work a line of tacking (basting) to mark the outline on the Hardanger fabric.

2 Find the centre of the design, match to the centre of the fabric and work in cross stitch over two blocks of the Hardanger fabric, from this point outwards following the chart.

3 Pin, tack (baste) and either machine or hand stitch the red satin ribbon into place (as shown on the chart) with a matching sewing thread.

4 Work out your chosen name in pencil on a piece of graph paper using the alphabet provided on page 77. Find the centre of your name and match to the centre of the linen band. Work outwards from this point following your chart. Work the top four lines in red DMC 321; the next four lines in sage-green DMC 732; and the last six lines in dark green DMC 934.

5 When all the embroidery has been completed and the ribbon sewn into place, trim the excess fabric to within ½in (13mm) of the line of tacking (basting) to allow for the seam.

6 With wrong sides together, fold the short red chintz strip (8½ × 1in/215 × 25mm), long sides to middle and tack (baste).

7 Pin and tack (baste) this strip ½in (13mm) away from the bottom edge of the embroidered name on the linen band.

8 With wrong sides facing, pin, tack (baste) and either machine or hand stitch the linen band complete with chintz edge to the top edge of the embroidered stocking, using a matching sewing thread and stitching close to the edges.

9 Pin the stocking shape, with wrong sides together, on to the red cotton chintz and cut this fabric to match.

10 Fold the white lining fabric in half widthwise, pin the stocking shape on to it and cut out the two lining pieces.

11 Place the embroidered stocking front and the red chintz backing right sides together. Pin, tack (baste) and either machine or hand stitch together ½in (13mm) away from the edge. Trim to within ¼in (6mm) of the stitching. Oversew by hand, or zig-zag on the sewing machine for strength. Turn the right way and iron the seam flat.

12 Slip stitch the green cord edging to the seam of the stocking using small stitches in a matching thread.

13 Pin, tack (baste) and either machine or hand stitch the two white cotton lining pieces together. Trim the excess fabric, oversew or zig-zag. Do not turn inside out. Slip the lining inside the stocking and tack (baste) the top edges together.

14 Pin and tack (baste) the long red chintz strip (16½ × 1in/419 × 25mm), right sides together with the top of the stocking, beginning in the middle at the back. Fold the short ends back on themselves so that they just meet. Machine or hand stitch ¼in (6mm) away from the edge. Make a ¼in (6mm) turning on the opposite edge of this binding strip, wrong sides facing and fold over the top of the stocking, concealing all the raw edges. Tack (baste) and then stitch into place using small hem stitches.

15 Finally, make a hanging loop from the 7 × 2½in (178 × 64mm) length of chintz by folding in half lengthways, right sides together. Pin, tack (baste) and either machine or hand stitch ¼in (6mm) from the edge on two sides. Turn and fold in the remaining edges. Close this opening with small stitches. Press flat. Pin in position across the top left corner of the stocking and stitch down firmly, making sure that you do not stitch the sides of the stocking together.

Alternatives

1 Omit the linen band and work the name over one block of Hardanger fabric at the top of the stocking. Edge with four lines of cross stitch in red.

2 Replace the holly motif with any of the other motifs of a similar size in the book eg Folk-art Reindeer, or a design such as the Stencil Santa on page 70.

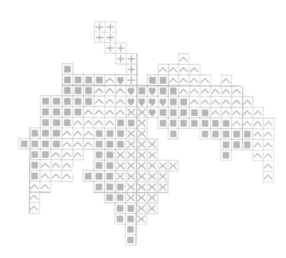

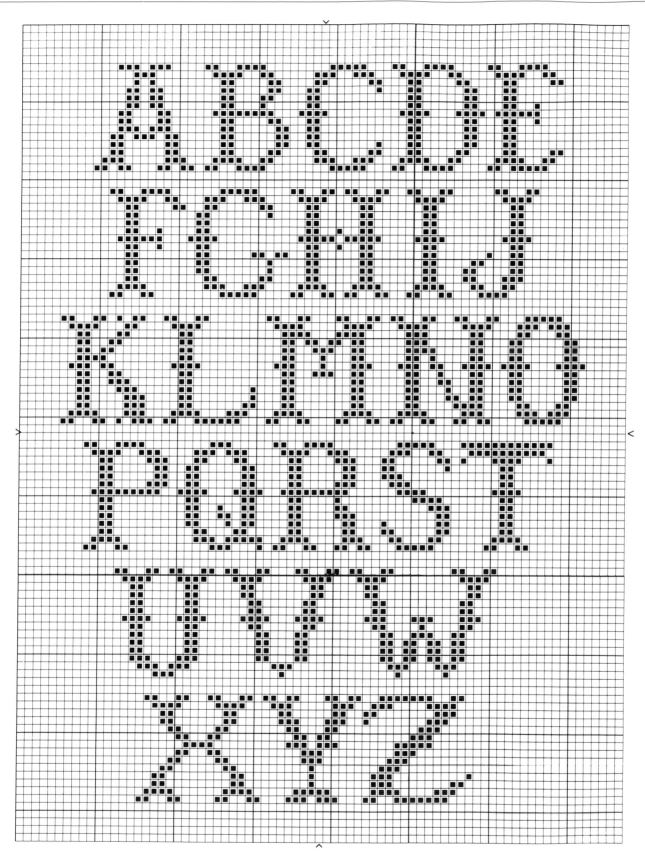

Holly Stocking

Holly Stocking

■	Dark green	934
♥	Bright red	321
∧	Mid green	3051
✕	Sage green	732
+	Dark brown	838

Dark vertical lines show
position of ribbon

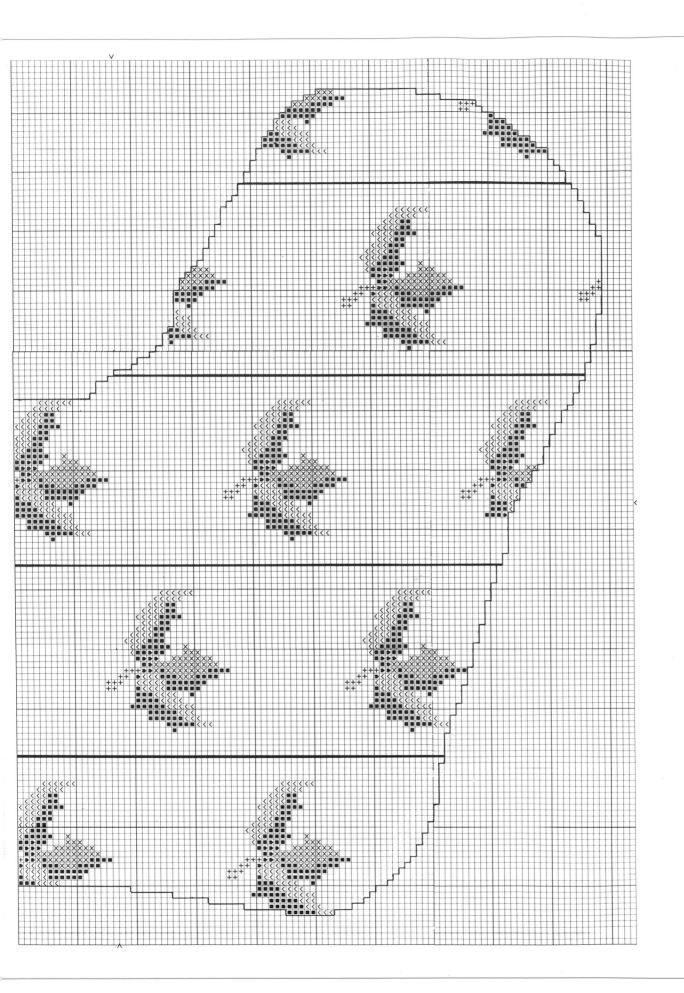

THREE WISE MEN

'Follow, follow, follow the star,
Caspar, Melchior and Balthazar'

This rich and vibrant cross stitch picture shows the three wise men bearing their gifts of gold, frankincense and myrrh. Worked in one strand of DMC black stranded cotton (floss) over one block of white Hardanger fabric that has been dyed with inks, the picture has been framed in a simple-to-make fabric-covered and decorated frame.

Design size: 7½in × 4in (190 × 102mm)
Stitch count: 94 × 163

❀ ❀

7½ × 10in (190 × 254mm) white 22-count Hardanger
   fabric
Red and blue ink
DMC black stranded cotton (floss) 310
6 × 9in (152 × 229mm) piece strong cardboard
10 × 12in (254 × 305mm) piece strong cardboard
Piece of shiny red fabric
Terylene wadding (batting)
Fine gold cord
Various sequins, shiny threads, gold braid
Glue/impact adhesive
10 × 12in (254 × 305mm) piece of black felt for
   backing
Small paint brush (or a piece of sponge or kitchen towel)
Three small mixing pots for the inks

1 Begin by soaking your fabric in lukewarm water. Do not rub or wring. Lay the wet fabric on a draining board covered with a sheet of polythene (an old carrier bag is ideal). Do not use newspaper, as the print dye may stain the fabric.

2 In each container, place a small amount of water (a few tablespoons). Add some red ink to the first one, blue to the second and a small amount of red and blue ink combined to the third. Using a brush or sponge apply the red ink wash to the top of the fabric, followed by the purple in the centre and then the blue nearer the bottom. Let the colours run into each other and leave until thoroughly dry.

3 Find the centre of the design (overleaf), match to the centre of the dyed fabric and, using the black cotton (floss), work outwards from this point, following the chart.

4 When the cross stitching is complete, attach the fine gold cord for reins, working a large back stitch over the mouth of each camel and then running a

long length as shown by the crosses in the chart from the mouth of each camel to the hand of their rider. Secure each length at the back of the work.

5 Mount the completed embroidery by lacing on to the smaller piece of card (see Finishing Techniques).

6 Cut an oblong aperture measuring 5½in × 8in (140 × 203mm) in the large piece of card. Using this as a template, draw around and cut out the terylene wadding (batting). Glue the wadding (batting) lightly to the card mount. Cover the padded frame with the shiny red fabric (see Finishing Techniques) and decorate with the gold braid, sequins and shiny threads as shown in the picture. (Pin in position first and when you are happy with the effect, use the adhesive to secure the braid and threads at the back of the frame. Use a tiny amount of adhesive for the sequins or stitch into position.)

7 Glue the black felt to the back of the work and using a small piece of gold cord, make a loop for hanging. Stitch this to the back of the work at the top.

Alternatives

1 Use a conventional frame and several card mounts to house the design.

2 Add the words 'Follow the star' etc, using one of the alphabets (see Alternative Alphabets, pages 118–19).

3 Work the cross stitch in DMC gold thread on a dark-coloured Aida fabric or linen. Frame in a padded velvet-covered mount with additions as shown.

Three Wise Men

CHRISTMAS MOTIFS SAMPLER

Worked on a dark unbleached linen in traditional Christmas colours, this fun to work sampler in cross stitch, back stitch, lazy daisy stitch and French knots is sure to be displayed with pride. Use two strands of cotton (floss) throughout.

Design size: 6½ × 4¼in (165 × 108mm)
Stitch count: 82 × 54

---

10 × 8in (254 × 203mm) unbleached Dublin linen, 25
  threads per inch (25mm)
DMC stranded cottons (floss) as shown in the key
  (page 88)

1 Find the centre of the design and work outwards from this point following the chart (page 88).

2 The cross and back stitches are worked over two threads of linen. Work all of the cross stitches first and then outline in back stitch where indicated – the stockings and puddings in 3371 dark brown and the word 'noel' in 890 dark green.

3 The ribbons and bows on the parcel motifs are worked in long stitch (horizontally and vertically) in 321 red. The bow consists of two lazy daisy stitches and two straight stitches (see the chart for placement).

4 Work two French knots in red 321 on top of each pudding as shown on the chart.

5 Frame as shown in the picture or see alternatives below.

Alternatives

The many motifs from this sampler can be used in a number of different ways, either individually or in groups.
  The possibilities are wide-ranging, as can be seen. The secret is to vary the use of fabric colour and

thread count. When this is done, a great variety of effects can be achieved and by choosing different ways of framing and displaying, many small projects can be completed quickly and simply, making them a perfect choice for Christmas fairs or as additional small gifts. Use your imagination to conjure up your own versions of those shown here.

1 Combine a few of the motifs to make a small Christmas hanging.

2 Work motifs individually and frame using small brass frames to make tree decorations. For added effect add a small bow in an appropriate colour.

3 Work one of the motifs on perforated paper together with a person's name for use as a special gift tag (use the alternative alphabet chart on page 118).

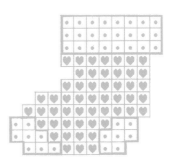

Further projects using motifs from the Christmas Motif Sampler

The possibilities are wide-ranging, as can be seen. The secret is to vary the use of fabric colour and thread count. When this is done, a great variety of effects can be achieved and by choosing different ways of framing and displaying, many small projects can be completed quickly and simply, making them a perfect choice for Christmas fairs or as additional small gifts. Use your imagination to conjure up your own versions of those shown here.

Christmas Motifs Sampler

■	Dark green	890	✕	Light green	703	♥ Bright red 321
◢	Green	910	•	Ecru		▲ Dark brown 3371

ADVENT CALENDAR

This unusual Advent calendar (overleaf) is much more versatile and so much more fun than a commercial version. Once worked it will be used and admired for years to come. The numerals are worked with DMC perlé (5) cotton variegated thread and the pockets are then made up individually before being sewn to a backing of Floba fabric, which gives the country feel. Wooden curtain draw rods are used for hanging, and huge tassels complete the particularly eye-catching effect.

Size: 36 × 23½in (914 × 597mm)

❋ ❋ ❋ ❋ ❋ ❋ ❋ ❋ ❋ ❋ ❋ ❋ ❋ ❋ ❋ ❋ ❋ ❋ ❋ ❋

20 × 27in (508 × 686mm) unbleached Dublin linen, 25 threads per inch (25mm)
DMC perlé cotton (5) red variegated 115
20 × 33in (508 × 838mm) small-print Christmas cotton fabric (for lining pockets)
9½yd (8.68m) green bias binding
One 36 × 25in (914 × 635mm) and two 6 × 25in (152 × 635mm) pieces of natural 18-count Floba fabric
36 × 25in (914 × 635mm) green cotton chintz fabric (for backing)
Matching sewing thread
2 pairs of wooden draw rods 27½in (700mm)
Masking tape (or similar, for binding the rods together)
2 large purchased tassels (or make your own, see Finishing Techniques)
4 Christmas buttons (optional)
30in (762mm) green cord
Impact adhesive/glue

1 Cut the unbleached Dublin linen into twenty-four 5 × 4½in (127 × 114mm) pieces.

2 Find the centre of each charted numeral (overleaf) and match to the centre of each square of fabric following the chart. Using the red variegated thread work outwards from this point.

3 When all twenty-four numerals are complete, cut the Christmas print fabric into twenty-four 5 × 5½in (127 × 140mm) pieces. Place the print fabric wrong sides together with the embroidered linen pieces and tack (baste) together so that the opening and overlap is at the top. Make a ¼in (6mm) turning on the overlap piece and fold

over the top of the linen. Pin, tack (baste) and either machine or hand stitch this ¾in (19mm) turning into place.

4 Make a small tuck at the bottom middle of each lined piece and secure with a few tacking (basting) stitches. Pin, tack (baste) and either machine or hand stitch the green bias binding around the edge of each pocket approximately ¼in (6mm) in from the edge, making sure that the top edges are turned under neatly. Fold the binding over the edges and hem stitch into place.

5 When all the pockets have been completed in this way, arrange them evenly on the large piece of Floba fabric as shown in the picture, leaving a gap of 3½in (89mm) top and bottom of the fabric. Pin into place. Tack (baste) and either machine or hem stitch each pocket to the backing close to the edge of each pocket.

6 Place the green chintz backing fabric right sides together with the whole pocketed piece. Pin, tack (baste) and either machine or hand stitch the two *side* edges together. Trim and either oversew this seam by hand or zig-zag stitch on a sewing machine, before turning and pressing.

7 Make ¼in (6mm) turnings on all of the long edges on the two remaining Floba strips and tack (baste). Fold the strips in half lengthways and press. Place the folded strips over the top and bottom ends of the lined piece, overlapping by 1in (25mm). Turn in the short ends. Pin, tack

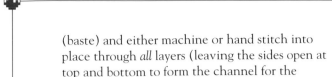

(baste) and either machine or hand stitch into place through *all* layers (leaving the sides open at top and bottom to form the channel for the wooden rods to pass through). Press flat.

8 Sew on a Christmas button in each corner as shown.

9 Saw off about 2in (51mm) from the ends of the wooden draw rods without the finial. Place two rods together with a finial at each end and when you have adjusted the length so that the finials just extend either side of the material channels, bind together in the middle with masking tape. Repeat with the second set of rods and pass one set through each of the channels.

10 Finally, slip the tassels on to the extended finials on the bottom set of rods and tie the green cord to the top finials. Secure the ends of the cord with adhesive to make sure that they do not unravel. Fill the pockets with small gifts – tiny bags of sweets, toys, pencil sharpeners, erasers, pencils.

Alternatives

1 Choose an alternative colourway for the project, ie, white linen with green numerals.

2 Frame each of the numerals separately using purpose-made frames and hang on the tree.

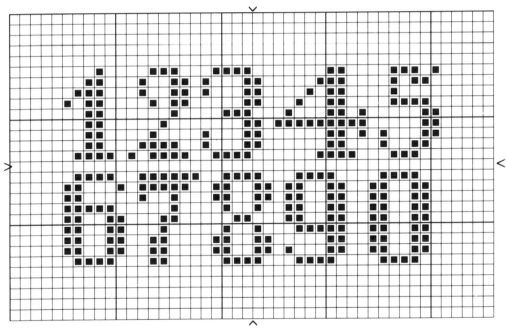

Advent Calendar (*work each cross stitch over 4 threads of linen*)

TARTAN HOOP

This charming little design – a simple tree motif with a bright tartan hoop frill – is worked in two strands of cotton (floss) over one block of dark green Aida fabric and outlined in DMC gold D282. Extremely quick and easy to make, it would brighten up any Christmas tree.

Design size: 2¼ × 1½in (57 × 38mm)
Stitch count: 30 × 21

✳ ✳

6 × 6in (152 × 152mm) dark green 14-count Aida fabric
DMC stranded cottons (floss) as shown on the chart
4in (102mm) diameter wooden embroidery hoop

For the hoop frill:

34 × 7in (864 × 178mm) tartan fabric
5 × 5in (127 × 127mm) dark green Christmas-print fabric
30in (762mm) of ¼in (6mm) gold ribbon
Matching sewing thread

1 Find the centre of the design and work outwards in cross stitch from this point following the chart.

2 When the design is complete, centre in the hoop and trim the embroidered fabric so that 1in (25mm) protrudes from the hoop frame.

3 Make the hoop frill from the tartan fabric (see page 124) and attach.

4 Cut a 4¾in (121mm) circle from the dark green Christmas fabric, make a ¼in (6mm) turning and tack (baste). Slip stitch the circle with wrong sides facing to the back of the hoop to cover the raw edges of the embroidered fabric.

5 Make two bows from the gold ribbon and stitch, with the smaller bow on top of the larger, to the bottom middle of the embroidery.

6 Finally, to hang the hoop, make a loop from a small piece of left-over ribbon (2in/51mm) and stitch it to the centre top at the back of the embroidery at the point where the backing fabric meets the tartan frill.

Alternatives

1 Make the hoop frill in a bright Christmas print.

2 Fill the space between the embroidered fabric and the backing with pine-scented pot-pourri.

3 Work the tree motif on perforated paper, cut to shape and add a loop at the back to make a simple tree decoration.

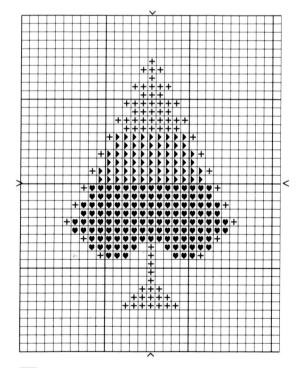

+	Gold thread	D282
▶	Light green	702
♥	Dark green	909

VICTORIAN INITIAL PICTURE AND PIN CUSHION

An elaborately framed initial makes a charming design for either a pin cushion worked in tent stitch with crewel wool on canvas, or a framed picture worked in stranded cotton (floss) on dark blue Aida fabric. Why not make one, or both of these delightful gifts for a special friend?

❊ ❊

For the Framed Initial:

Design size: 4 × 3¼in (102 × 82mm)
Stitch count: 53 × 46

6 × 6in (152 × 152mm) dark blue 14-count Aida fabric
DMC Ecru stranded cotton (floss)

1 Find the centre of your chosen initial (from the alphabet chart overleaf) and match to the centre of the design chart also on page 96). Mark the position of your initial lightly in pencil and match to the centre of the fabric.

2 Begin work at this point using two strands of cotton (floss) over one block of fabric. Complete the rest of the design from the chart.

For the Pin Cushion:

Size (of finished pin cushion): 4 × 3½in (102 × 89mm)
Stitch count: 53 × 46

5½ × 5½in (140 × 140mm) white 22-count petit point canvas
DMC Crewel wool (Medici), ecru and blue 8202
5½ × 5½in (140 × 140mm) blue cotton velvet fabric
DMC stranded cotton (floss) 924 antique blue (for the cord and tassels)
Polyester fibre for filling

1 Follow the instructions given for step 1 above but work the design in blue tent stitch with two strands of wool over one thread of canvas. Fill in the background with DMC ecru, working an additional four rows of tent stitch on each side of the design.

2 Place the completed embroidery and the velvet backing right sides together. Pin, tack (baste) and either machine or hand stitch together leaving a gap for turning. Remove the tacking (basting) stitches.

3 Turn right sides out and after filling with polyester fibre, close the opening with tiny stitches.

4 Make the cord and four tassels (see Finishing Techniques) from the stranded cotton (floss). Beginning at one of the corners, slip stitch the cord to the edge of the pin cushion using a matching thread. Stitch one tassel to each corner of the pin cushion, securing firmly.

Alternatives

1 Add a ribbon loop for hanging, and use the tiny cushions as tree ornaments.

2 Work the design on various items of clothing using waste canvas.

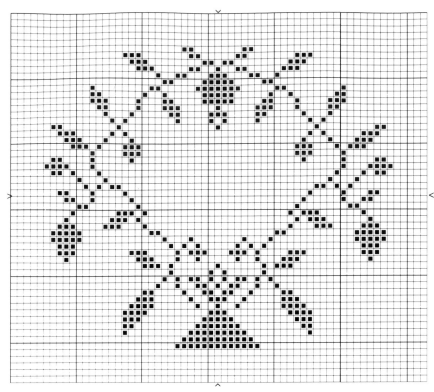

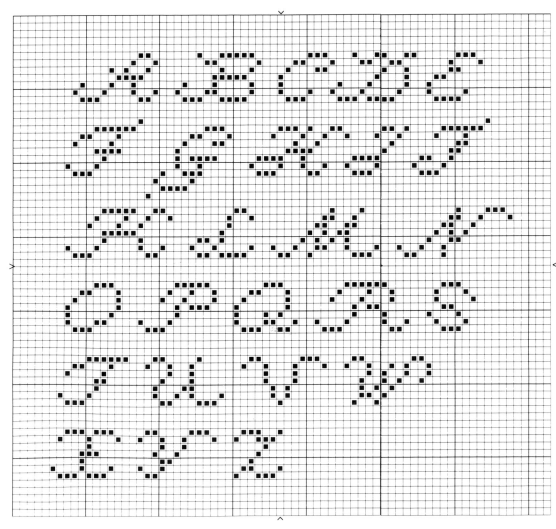

NAME PICTURES

Why not make one of these highly original name pictures for your favourite person (below and overleaf). Worked in cross stitch using two strands of cotton (floss) over one block of Aida fabric, the designs are simple, but lend a very personal touch to a special gift.

❀ ❀

Cream 14-count Aida fabric. (The size will depend on your chosen name. Follow steps 1 to 3 below. When your graph is complete, work out the size of the fabric required from the stitch count. Use the method shown on page 10 to calculate the size of fabric required.)
DMC stranded cotton (floss) in your chosen colours
Graph paper
Pencil

1 To work out the placement of the letters of your chosen name, first, draw a central line vertically in pencil on graph paper. Beginning with the top letter, count how many squares are used for that letter (from the chart given) and position an equal number of squares either side of the line.

2 Repeat this procedure (with the first two letters of the name) for the second line, leaving a gap of three squares in between each letter and also between the horizontal lines.

3 Repeat until the bottom line shows the complete name.

4 Find the centre of the design, match to the centre of the fabric and work outwards from this point using your chosen threads 'Thomas' was worked with DMC stranded cottons (floss) 336 dark blue, 349 red, 907 bright green. 'Katie' was worked with a space-dyed thread and the remaining 'shadow' letters were filled in with DMC 818 very pale pink.

Alternatives

1 Fill in the area surrounding the main design (ie the 'shadow' letters) with a different coloured thread as in the 'Katie' design. Simply complete the sequence of letters in the name to the desired size (working out on graph paper as before).

2 Use a different alphabet for the design. A small back stitch alphabet worked in bright, jewel-like colours would make a wonderful design for a card (see Alternative Alphabets page 118).

3 Use a Christmas message instead of a name, for example, Oh Holy Night, Merry Christmas.

4 Work the design in wool (woollen yarn) on a large-mesh canvas and make into a cushion.

Name Pictures

DECORATIVE FRAMES

This design (overleaf) shows just how versatile a simple border pattern can be. The border used on the two frames is exactly the same, but looks quite different due to the choice of fabric and threads. Both designs would make wonderful gifts. The mirror mount is worked with stranded cottons (floss) on Yorkshire Aida and the photograph mount is worked in stranded cottons (floss) with Marlitt viscose thread on cream Belfast linen.

For the Mirror Mount:

Design size: 10¼ × 6¾in (260 × 171mm)
Stitch count: 141 × 93

14 × 11in (356 × 279mm) grey/beige 14-count
   Yorkshire Aida fabric
DMC stranded cottons (floss) as shown in the key
26in (660mm) narrow piping cord
26in (660mm) purple bias binding
Piece of strong card 11 × 7¾in (279 × 197mm)
Glue/impact adhesive
Wooden frame to fit the mount (if you wish to display as
   shown in the picture)
9 × 6in (229 × 152mm) mirror

1 Measure 2in (51mm) down from the top of the fabric and 2in (51mm) in from the side. Begin working the top left hand corner of the border design here, following the chart.

2 Cut an oblong central aperture in the piece of card 7½ × 4¼in (190 × 108mm).

3 Make up the embroidered fabric as a mount (see Finishing Techniques page 122).

4 Fold the bias binding in half and place the piping cord on the fold on the wrong side of the binding, ie the inside. Either machine or hand stitch the two sides of the binding together as close as possible to the piping cord, enclosing it.

5 Starting at one of the corners, glue the covered cord around the inner edge of the fabric covered card, snipping the bias binding up to the cord at the corners, so that it lies flat with the frame. Trim the excess length to size, folding in the raw edges and gluing into place.

6 Position your mirror at the back of the mount and hold into place with masking tape.

7 Fit into your frame.

For the Photograph Mount:

Design size: 6 × 6in (152 × 152mm)
Stitch count 93 × 93

10 × 10in (254 × 254mm) cream Belfast linen,
   32 threads per inch (25mm)
DMC stranded cottons (floss) and Marlitt Viscose thread
   as shown in the key
16in (406mm) narrow piping cord
16in (406mm) pale-pink bias binding
Piece of strong card 6¾ × 6¾in (171 × 171mm)
Glue/impact adhesive
Wooden frame to fit the mount (if you wish to display as
   shown in the picture)
A photograph 5 × 5in (127 × 127mm)

Decorative Frames

Mirror			Photo		
■	Dark sage	730	■	Mid green	3052
×	Light sage	733	×	Light green	3348
♥	Dark purple	327	♥	Apricot	352
•	Light purple	3041	•	Cream (Marlitt 1013)	
S	Mid purple	553	S	Light rose	3064

Repeat instructions 1–7 as for the mirror mount, substituting a photograph for the mirror and altering sizes as follows:

Work only three repeat motifs on the side edges instead of five, as shown on the mirror mount. Cut a square central aperture in the card 3¾ × 3¾in (95 × 95mm).

Alternatives

1 Work the border pattern in a colour scheme of your own choosing and add a favourite verse instead of a photograph or mirror (the design then becomes a sampler).

2 Use the border pattern to decorate household linen, for example, towels, pillowcases, table linen.

3 Cut a smaller aperture for the photograph mount, leaving enough room for a person's name to be worked just above the bottom border. (Use a small back stitch alphabet – see Alternative Alphabets page 118.)

4 For a baby's photograph, add lace as an edging instead of covered cord.

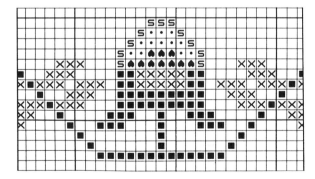

INITIALLED CUSHION WITH TASSELS

Why not work this charming gift cushion for a favourite friend personalised with his or her initial from the chart given on page 107. Worked in cross stitch in DMC Laine Colbert over one thread of lockweave canvas, this unique gift will be sure to please.

Design size: 7½ × 8in (190 × 203mm)
Stitch count: 76 × 80

❊ ❊

11 × 11in (279 × 279mm) white lockweave canvas, 10 holes per inch (25mm)
DMC Laine Colbert in colours as shown in the cushion and alphabet chart keys
DMC gold thread D282
10 × 10in (254 × 254mm) maroon cotton velvet fabric
Polyester filling
Matching sewing thread

1 Choose your initial from the alphabet chart (page 107) and position it in the centre of the canvas. Increase the size of the initial by treating every square as a block of four stitches.

2 Beginning at the mid-point, work your initial in cross stitch in DMC yellow-gold 7784 Laine Colbert over one thread of canvas. Do not separate the strands of the wool (woollen yarn), use as supplied. When your initial is complete, oversew each cross stitch with a half cross stitch worked diagonally from top right to bottom left in DMC gold thread D282.

3 Fill in the remaining background from the cushion chart given (page 106).

4 Trim the canvas to within ½in (13mm) of the embroidery.

5 Place the embroidery right side upwards on a clean surface. Place the velvet backing right side down over the embroidery and trim to size. Pin, tack (baste) and either machine or hand stitch together, leaving a 3in (76mm) gap for turning. Oversew or zig zag the seams to strengthen them.

6 Turn the cushion right sides out and fill with the polyester filling. Close the gap with small invisible stitches. Make a plaited braid from maroon, dark green and lime green wool (woollen yarn) using two very long lengths of each. Sew to the edge of the cushion where the velvet and embroidered canvas meet, using small invisible stitches.

7 Finally, make four tassels from the same coloured wool (see Finishing Techniques) and stitch one securely to each corner.

Alternatives

1 Work the design in half cross stitch over one thread of linen and use for a greetings card or frame as a miniature.

2 Work an initial from the alphabet chart, and use some of the borders in the design as a surround. Frame as a small picture.

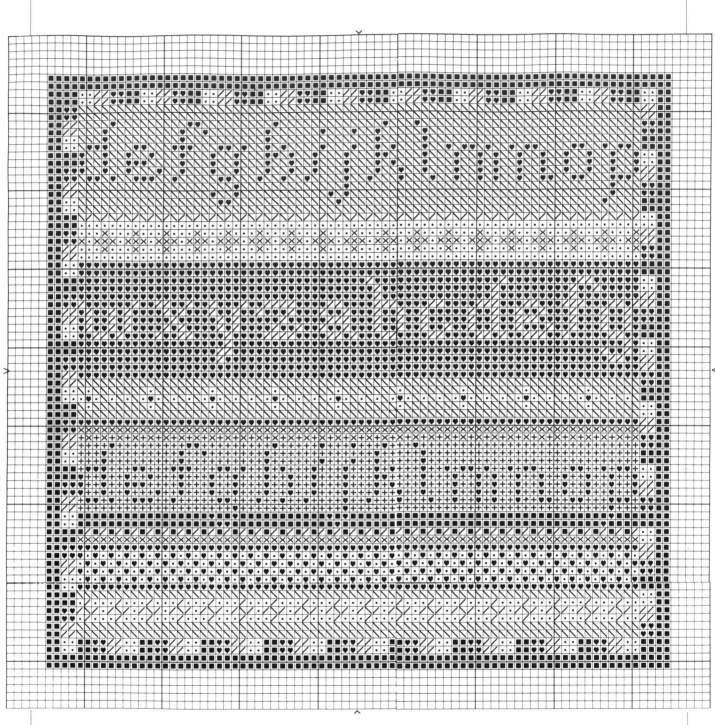

Initialled Cushion

■	Dark green	7398	◥	Blue	7288
•	Light grey	7302	✕	Mid green	7344
◤	Light green	7341	+	Holly green	7347
♥	Maroon	7219			

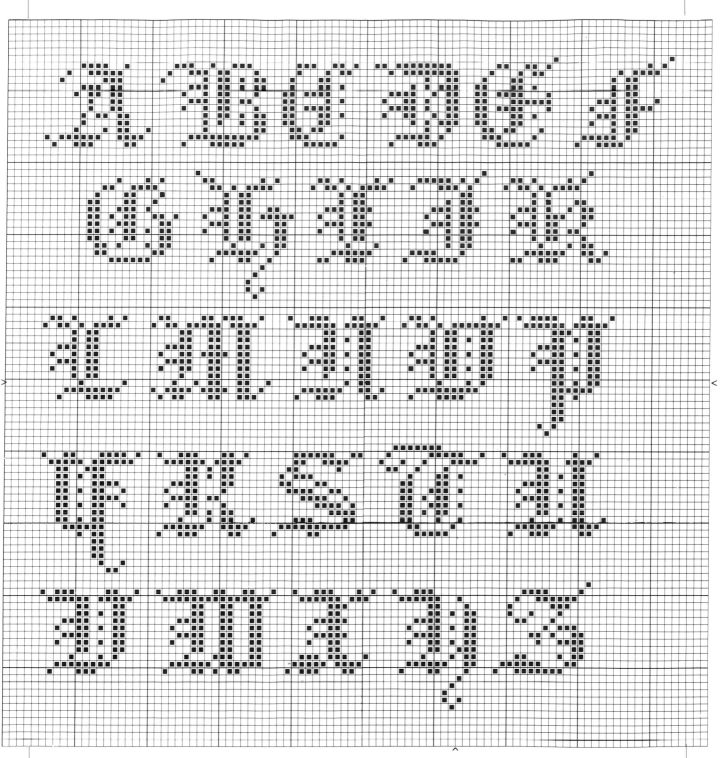

Initialled Cushion Alphabet

■ Gold 7784

ELEGANT ALPHABET

This elegant and stylish alphabet is extremely adaptable and can be used in many different ways to create wonderfully unique and totally original gifts. Here is just a small selection of how the alphabet can be used. (See also pages 114–15)

'H' was worked with red/brown space-dyed thread and DMC gold thread D282 in cross stitch over two threads of cream evenweave linen, 28 threads per inch (25mm). A square wooden frame has been used to complement the colours of the thread.

'B' was worked with DMC stranded cotton (floss) dark navy 823 2 strands and DMC gold thread D282 in cross stitch over two threads of cream evenweave linen, 28 threads per inch (25mm). Two mounts in toning colours were added to give the design impact and it was then framed in a simple navy-coloured frame.

'F' was worked with DMC stranded cotton (floss) 699 emerald green and DMC gold thread D282 in tent stitch over one thread of cream evenweave linen, 28 threads per inch (25mm). It was then displayed in a small gold frame.

'R' was worked with DMC stranded cotton (floss) 3064 pink/beige and DMC gold thread D282 in tent stitch over one thread of Belfast linen, 32 threads per inch (25mm). It was housed in a purchased trinket pot.

'L' was worked with DMC stranded cotton (floss) 995 aquamarine and DMC gold thread D282 in cross stitch over two threads of Belfast linen, 32 threads per inch (25mm). It was housed in a purchased free-standing gold frame.

'A' was worked in DMC stranded cotton (floss) 902 dark maroon and DMC gold thread D282 in cross stitch over two threads of cream evenweave linen, 28 threads per inch (25mm). It was framed in a small gold frame.

'E' was worked in DMC stranded cotton (floss) 333 dark lilac and DMC gold thread D282 in cross stitch over two threads of cream evenweave linen, 28 threads per inch (25mm). The design was then mounted on to a piece of card and lengths of decorative ribbon were glued around the edges to form a mount. The design was then housed in a purchased photograph frame.

'K' was worked in a variety of brightly coloured threads using varying lengths. Waste canvas was used to apply the design to the sweatshirt. Simply choose your initial, cut a piece of waste canvas 5 × 5in (127 × 127mm) and tack (baste) in position on your sweatshirt. Find the centre of your initial and match to the centre of the canvas. Work the design in cross stitch, working through the waste canvas and sweatshirt, following the chart and when completed, spray the whole design with water. Using tweezers, remove the soaked threads of the canvas one by one. Leave to dry and press on the wrong side of the embroidery.

Alternatives

1 Use an initial for a greetings card. (The design can then be framed if the recipient chooses to do so.)

2 Work an initial for each member of the family in tent stitch on a fine linen over one thread. Frame with a hoop frill (see Finishing Techniques) using a shiny gold fabric on tiny 4in (102mm) diameter wooden embroidery hoops. Add a hanging loop with ribbon or card. These would make wonderful decorations, adding a personal touch to your tree.

3 Using waste canvas (see 'K' above) work an initial on a T-shirt, blouse pocket, pillowcase, sheet, towel, cushion, apron, or any other item of clothing or household fabrics.

4 Work an initial to decorate a pin cushion. This would make a lovely gift for a fellow stitcher. Either use one of the wooden pin cushion bases that are available in needlecraft shops or simply make up as a tiny cushion.

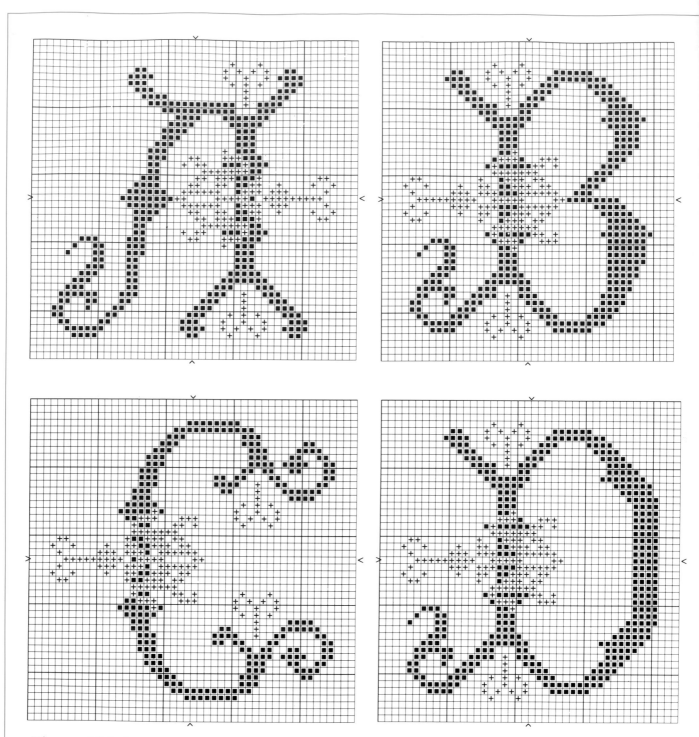

Elegant Alphabet

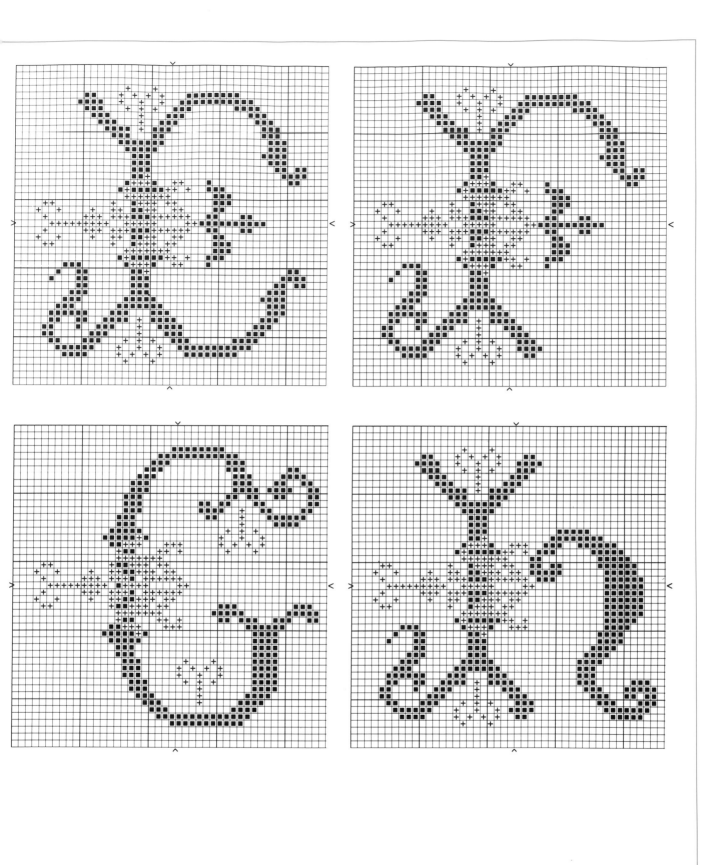

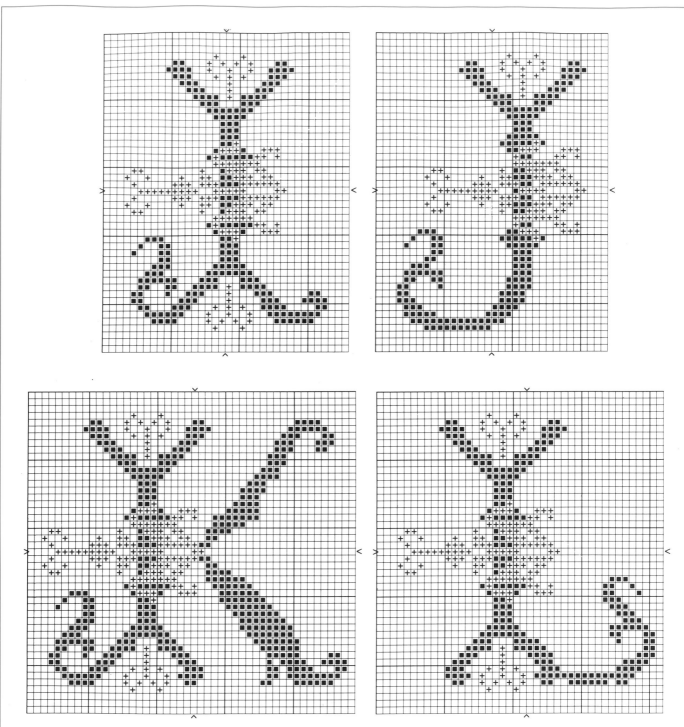

Elegant Alphabet

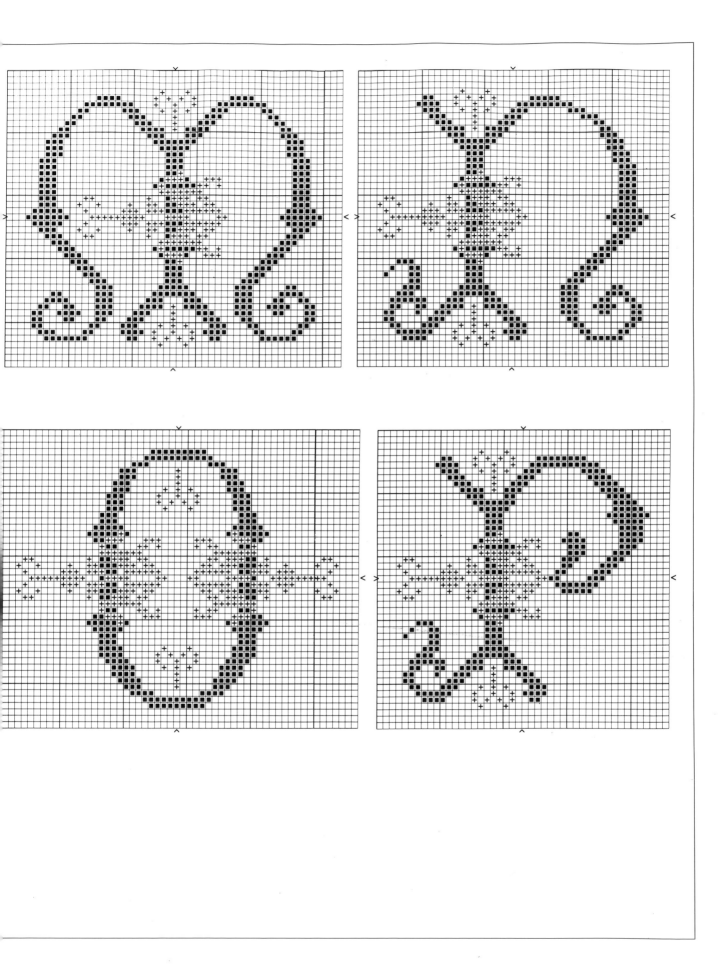

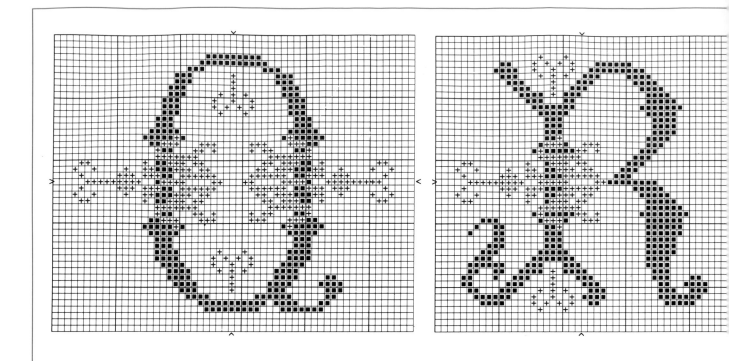

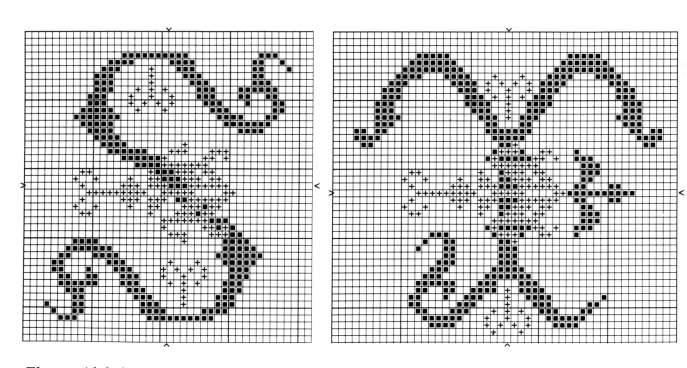

Elegant Alphabet

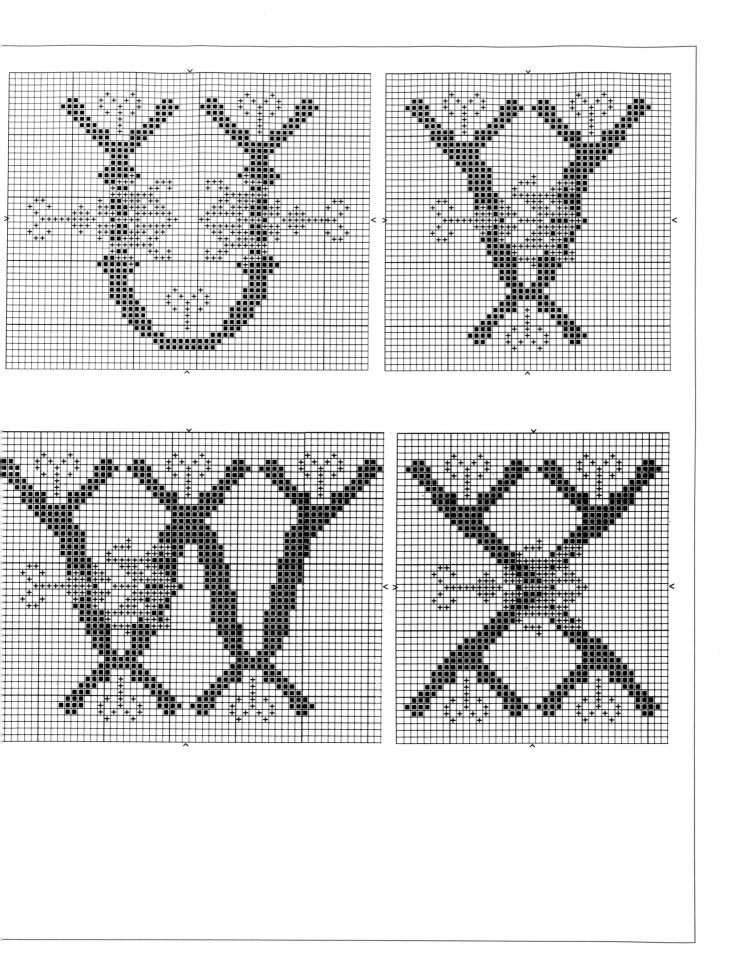

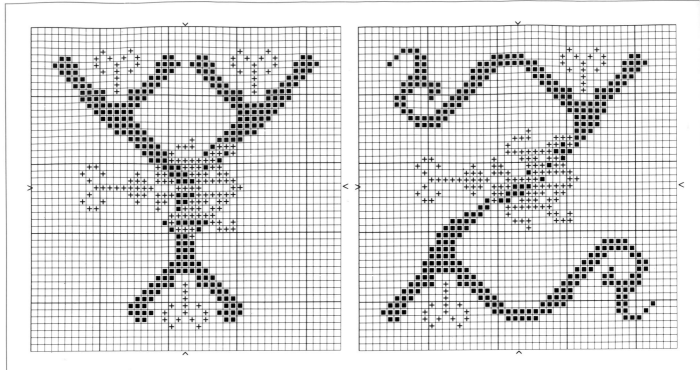

Elegant Alphabet

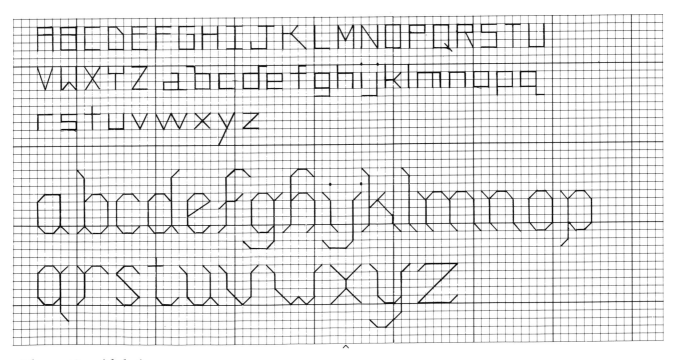

Alternative Alphabets

Alternative Alphabets

STITCH DIRECTORY

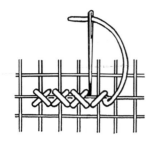

Cross stitch over one thread

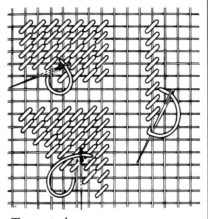

Tent stitch

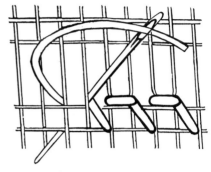

Hem stitch

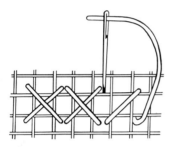

Cross stitch over two threads

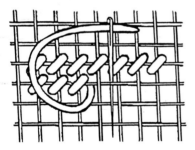

Half cross stitch

Lazy Daisy

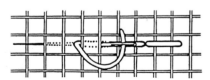

Back stitch

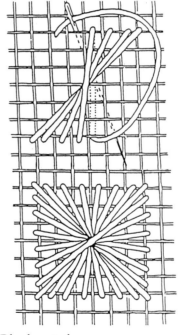

Rhodes stitch

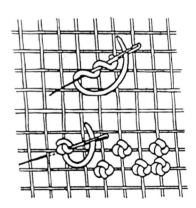

French knot

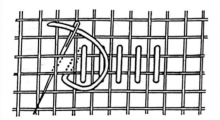

Satin stitch Long/Straight Stitch
(really just one satin stitch)

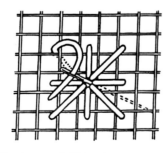

Eyelet stitch/Algerian eye

FINISHING TECHNIQUES

Before taking your embroidery to the framers or framing it yourself, it is advisable to run through the following check list.

1 It is easy to miss out stitches or even whole areas of a design, so always make a point of checking the completed design against the chart.

2 Turn your work over and check for loose, trailing threads. Check that the threads are secure then snip off as close to the work as possible. Dark-coloured trailing threads in particular will show through light fabric and spoil the appearance of the finished work.

3 Unless your work has become really grubby in the working, avoid washing and ironing. Embroidery *always* looks better without this process. If you have taken the necessary steps to protect it while in progress, and have used an embroidery frame or hoop (one that is large enough to encompass not only the work but also to allow a reasonable margin for framing), and taken the trouble to store it in a clean white pillowcase, for example, when not in use, then washing should not be necessary. If, however, it is necessary, wash by hand, in lukewarm water with mild soap flakes, taking great care not to rub or wring. Simply swish the embroidery about in the water. Rinse well, then roll in a clean white towel. Open out and leave to dry. To press, lay several layers of towelling on an ironing board. Lay the work face down on the towels, cover with a clean white cloth and press with a warm iron. This method prevents the stitches from becoming flattened. Do not iron plastic canvas or perforated paper.

Stretching and Mounting Your Work

This part of the finishing process is vital as the most wonderful piece of work can be totally ruined if it is puckered or creased. It is *always* worth going to the trouble of finishing your work properly by stretching and mounting (unless it is *very* tiny indeed). (As linen is often stitched on a frame, a gentle ironing on the wrong side may sometimes be sufficient.)

1 Use a strong, acid-free mount board (available from good art shops) or hardboard (covered with acid-free paper). Measure your work and cut the board slightly bigger than your embroidery if a mount is to be used or, if not, to the size of your chosen frame.

2 Place the card or covered hardboard on the wrong side of the embroidery and when in position, secure with straight pins inserted into the edge. Turn frequently to check that the embroidery remains correctly placed.

3 Fold over the side edges of the fabric, then use a long length of strong thread (fine crochet cotton is ideal) to lace back and forth (Fig 1a). Pull up the stitches to tighten and secure firmly.

4 Complete the top and bottom in the same way (Fig 1b).

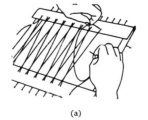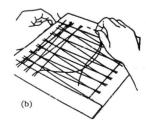

(a)   (b)

Fig 1 Lacing technique for mounting your work

Fabric-Covered Mounts

The technique of covering mounts with fabric means that you need not limit yourself to plain, uninteresting mounts. Virtually any colour, pattern or texture is possible with this method. You will need: strong card, fabric, glue/impact adhesive, a metal rule, a scalpel or craft knife, and a cutting board or several layers of card to protect the surface you are cutting on. If you are making a padded mount (as in the Three Wise Men project), you will also need one or two layers of terylene wadding (batting).

Covering a Mount with Fabric

1 Measure the completed embroidery carefully and cut the mount and the aperture to the size required. Round and oval apertures are very difficult to cut perfectly, and even though you are covering with fabric, uneven edges will show. Unless you are very skilled it is best to ask your picture framer to cut these for you.

2 Cut the fabric to the size of the mount *plus* allowances for turnings (the allowances will vary according to the size of the mount and also the type of fabric chosen, ie because of its thickness, velvet will require a larger allowance than fine cotton). Always make sure that you align the mount with the straight grain of the fabric.

3 Place the fabric right side down and position the mount in the middle. (If making a padded mount, cut the padding to the same size as the mount and place between the fabric and the card.) Snip off the corners of the fabric as shown by the dotted lines in the diagram below.

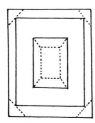 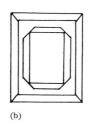

(a) (b)

Fig 2 Covering a mount with fabric

4 Apply adhesive to the remaining fabric at the outer edge. Fold over and press flat.

5 To cut out the inside 'window', first cut out the rectangle as shown by the dotted line (Fig 2a) and then carefully snip into the corners, stopping just short of the edge. Apply adhesive to this remaining fabric, fold over and press flat (Fig 2b).

6 Add any further embellishments which may be required – bows, sequins, braids and then carefully align the mount over the embroidery. Fix with glue or masking tape.

Framing

The correct choice of frame can, quite simply, make or break a piece of work. A relatively simple piece can be greatly enhanced or even transformed with a carefully chosen frame and/or mount. It is important, therefore not to rush this process, but to take some time to consider all the possibilities. You may have spent many hours on the work to be framed, so it would be sacrilege at this stage to spoil it with an inappropriate frame.

You need not go to great expense, often a coat of paint is all that is needed to transform a relatively dull frame. Try painting in bright primary colours or, to achieve pastel colours with a stippled effect, simply paint the frame in one colour, then dip an old toothbrush in a contrasting colour and run your finger along the bristles to flick the paint on to the frame (be sure to protect the surrounding areas with plenty of newspaper!). For a 'limed' effect, first paint the frame in your chosen colour and when dry rub a little ready-mixed Polyfilla into the grain and corner joins, wiping off the excess. When dry, finish with a coat of matt varnish. There are also many coloured varnishes available that will greatly enhance a plain frame. Try matching one to the main colour of your design.

Unless your work has a very raised surface or is very textured, the use of glass is advisable as this will protect the work from dust, dirt and inquisitive fingers! You will need to choose between plain or non-reflective glass. Non-reflective glass sounds the obvious choice, but often has a rather mottled and flat appearance which tends to dull colours. If you decide to use glass but are not using a mount, ask your picture framer to use thin strips of card to prevent the glass coming into contact with your needlework. This will prevent it from flattening your stitches.

Making a Fold-over Card

A great variety of ready-made fold-over cards are now available from art and needlework shops (see suppliers in Acknowledgements). If, however, the size or colour you want is not available, the following instructions will enable you to make your own.

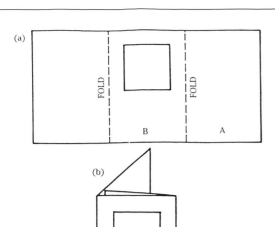

Fig 3 How to make a fold over card

1 Choose thin card in a colour to match your design.

2 Measure your embroidery to assess the size and shape of the aperture. (Round, oval and heart-shaped apertures are much more difficult to cut accurately unless you have great skill.) Do not attempt to cut any aperture with scissors, always use a craft knife or scalpel.

3 Cut your card to the size and shape required (Fig 3a). Cut an aperture in the middle section 'B' and using a craft knife, lightly score fold lines as indicated by the dotted lines.

4 Position the aperture over your embroidery. Trim away any excess fabric and glue into position or secure with double-sided sticky tape.

5 Fold 'A' over 'B' and glue together (Fig 3b).

How to make a Tassel

1 Cut a piece of stiff card to the length you wish the tassel to be. Wind the thread around the card until the required thickness is achieved. (If you are making a set of tassels, keep count of the number of times you wind around the card, so all the tassels will be the same.)

2 Thread a needle with a long piece of the same colour thread. Pass it under the wound threads at the top, next to the card and tie securely leaving

two trailing threads of the same length. Do not fasten off.

3 Cut the bound threads at the bottom of the card to release them.

4 Thread both of the ends used to tie the tassel into the needle, pass through the top of the tassel and bring out about ½in (13mm) down (less for a smaller tassel).

5 Wind the thread tightly several times around the tassel to form the head. Knot securely and pass the needle back through the bound threads to the top. Attach with this remaining thread to the article.

How to make a Twisted Cord

1 Assess the length of cord required and cut a length of thread three times as long.

2 Make a loop in each end of the thread and attach one end to a hook or doorknob.

3 Slip a pencil through the other end and keeping the thread taut, begin twisting the pencil round and round until, when relaxed, the thread begins to twist back on itself.

4 Keeping the threads taut, fold the length in half, matching the ends together. Stroke along the cord to even out the twists. Finally, tie the ends together. If a thicker cord is required, simply use more strands.

Charting Names and Dates

If you wish to personalise your work, for example by adding a name and date, this is relatively easy to do.

Work out your details in pencil on graph paper, adjusting the spacing to suit the letters chosen. For example, a lower case i placed next to a lower case l usually looks better with two spaces between if the alphabet is very plain (even if only one space is allowed between the other letters). This type of adjustment will sometimes be necessary between other letters but this will quickly become apparent during the charting process.

When you have worked out your details, count the number of squares used vertically and horizontally and position the lettering evenly and centrally in the appropriate place on your fabric.

How to make a Gathered Hoop Frill

1 Cut your fabric 7in (178mm) wide × twice the circumference of the hoop plus 6in (152mm). You can vary these measurements – for a very full frill add extra material allowance to the length and width, for a narrower frill, shorten the width slightly (but make sure that the length is as above).

2 If you are adding lace, cut to the same length as the fabric.

3 Make folds as shown in Fig 4a and press.

4 Tack (baste) the lace to the raw edge of the fabric (right side facing) and fold as shown in Fig 4b.

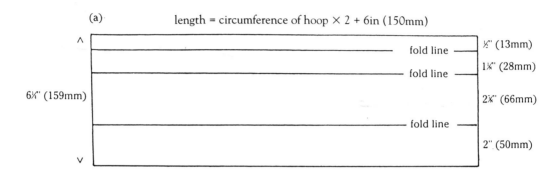

(a)

length = circumference of hoop × 2 + 6in (150mm)

fold line — ½" (13mm)

fold line — 1¼" (28mm)

6¼" (159mm)

2¾" (66mm)

fold line —

2" (50mm)

Fig 4 How to make a hoop frill

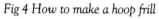

(b)

take lace to raw edge of fabric

(c)

fabric

lace

Tack through ALL layers on dotted line.

5 Fold again as shown in Fig 4c and then pin, tack (baste) and machine or hand stitch through all layers close to the fold as shown in Fig 4d.

6 Unscrew the hoop and slot the outer part through the fabric frill as shown. Replace the screw, but do not tighten fully. Ease on to the inner frame which has the embroidery positioned over it. Adjust the screw until the outer frame will just fit over the embroidery. Ease the frill, adjusting the gathers until they are evenly distributed. Make a small turning on one edge and oversew to the remaining edge. Finish the hoop with ribbon bows, silk or dried flowers, holly etc, positioning them so that they hide the join of the frill. Attach with small stitches in a matching thread.

7 Make a small hoop with ribbon for hanging and attach to the back of the fabric frill at the top with small stitches.

(d)

pin, tack & machine through all layers close to edge of fold

slot hoop through here

lace

fabric

THREAD CONVERSION CHART

DMC	ANCHOR	DMC	ANCHOR	DMC	ANCHOR	DMC	ANCHOR	DMC	ANCHOR	DMC	ANCHOR	DMC	ANCHOR	DMC	ANCHOR
BLANC	1	372	854	581	28*	738	361	825	162	924	851	992	187*	3685	69
ECRU	387	400	351	597	168*	739	366	826	161*	926	850	993	186*	3687	68
208	111	402	347	598	167*	740	316*	827	9159*	927	848	995	410	3688	66
209	109	407	914*	600	78	741	314	828	158*	928	847	996	433	3689	49
210	108	413	401	601	77	742	303	829	906	930	922	3011	845	3705	35
211	342	414	235	602	63	743	305	830	277*	931	921	3012	843	3706	33
221	897	415	398	603	62	744	301	831	277*	932	343	3013	842	3708	31
223	895*	420	374	604	55	745	300*	832	907*	934	862*	3021	905*	3712	10*
224	893	422	943	605	50	746	386	833	(907)*	935	269*	3022	(899)*	3713	968*
225	892	433	371	606	335	747	928	834	874	936	846	3023	(899)*	3716	25
300	352	434	365	608	333	754	4146*	838	380	937	268*	3024	900*	3721	896*
301	349*	435	901*	610	889	758	868*	839	360*	938	381	3031	360*	3722	895*
304	47	436	363	611	898	760	9*	840	379	939	152	3032	903*	3726	970
307	289	437	362	612	832	761	23	841	378	943	188	3033	830	3727	969*
309	42	444	291	613	853	762	234	842	376	945	881	3041	871	3731	(38)
310	403	445	288	632	936	772	259	844	273*	946	332	3042	870	3733	75*
311	148	451	233	640	393*	775	128	869	944	947	330	3045	888	3740	872
312	979	452	232	642	392	776	24	890	(683)	948	778*	3046	887	3743	869
315	(896)*	453	231	644	396	778	968*	891	29	950	4146*	3047	886	3746	118*
316	969*	469	267*	645	273*	780	310	892	28	951	880	3051	861	3747	120
317	400	470	266*	646	8581*	781	309*	893	27	954	203	3052	859*	3750	(123)
318	399	471	265	647	8581*	782	308	894	26	955	206*	3053	858*	3752	976
319	(217)	472	(278)	648	900*	783	307	895	269*	956	54	3064	883	3753	975
320	215	498	(43)	666	46	791	178	898	359	957	52	3072	274	3755	140
321	9046	500	879	676	891	792	177	899	(40)	958	187*	3078	292	3756	158*
322	978	501	878	677	300*	793	176	900	(326)*	959	186*	3325	129	3760	161*
326	59	502	877	680	901*	794	175	902	72	961	76	3326	36	3761	9159*
327	100	503	876	699	229	796	133	904	258	962	75*	3328	10*	3765	169*
333	119	504	875	700	228	797	132	905	257	963	73	3340	329	3766	167*
334	977	517	170	701	227	798	131	906	256	964	185	3341	328	3768	779
335	(41)	518	(168)*	702	226	799	145	907	255	966	240	3345	268*	3770	276
336	149	519	(167)*	703	239	800	144	909	923	970	324*	3346	267*	3772	914*
340	118*	520	862*	704	283	801	358	910	230*	971	316*	3347	266*	3773	882
341	117	522	860	712	926	806	169*	911	230*	972	298	3348	264	3774	778*
347	13*	523	859*	718	88	807	168*	912	205	973	290	3350	65	3776	349*
349	13*	524	858*	720	326*	809	130	913	204	975	370	3354	74	3777	20
350	(11)	535	(273)*	721	324*	813	160	915	972	976	(309)*	3362	263	3778	9575
351	10*	543	933	722	323	814	45	917	89	977	313	3363	262	3779	868*
352	9*	550	101	725	306	815	22	918	341*	986	246	3364	260	3781	905*
353	6	552	99	726	295	816	(44)	919	340	987	244	3371	382	3782	831
355	341*	553	98	727	293	817	19	920	339	988	243	3607	87	3787	(393)*
356	5975	554	97	729	890	818	48	921	338	989	242	3608	86	3790	903*
367	(216)	561	212	730	924*	819	271	922	337	991	(189)	3609	85	3799	236
368	214	562	210	731	281*	820	134								
369	(213)	563	208	732	281*	822	390								
370	856	564	206*	733	280*	823	150								
371	855	580	924*	734	279	824	164								

Indicates shades used more than once

BIBLIOGRAPHY

American Country Christmas Oxmoor House Inc (1992)

The Christmas Book (*The Best of Good Housekeeping at Christmas* 1922–1962) Ebury Press (1988)

The Christmas Crafts Book Search Press (1979)

Cirker, Blanche (Ed) *Needlework Alphabets and Designs* Dover Publications (1975)

Colby, Averil *Samplers* Batsford (1964)

Dimbleby Josceline *The Josceline Dimbleby Christmas Book* Sainsbury's (1987)

Lawrence, Francine (Ed) *Country Christmas* Ebury Press (1990)

Miller, Dennis *Christmas Customs* Ladybird Books (1988)

Mulherin, Jennifer *The Little Book of Christmas* Salamander Books Ltd (1990)

The Oxford Christmas Carol Book Oxford University Press (1988)

Pesel, Louisa, F. *Historical Designs for Embroidery* Batsford (1956)

Segall, Barbara *The Holly and the Ivy* Ebury Press (1991)

ACKNOWLEDGEMENTS

I would very much like to thank the following people for their help and support:

My husband Chris, for confirming that I am still his favourite author in spite of the fact that our home has resembled a grotto for the last twelve months!; my children Nicholas and Katie who seem to like the grotto and have forgiven me for not returning to normal as promised when the last book *Alphabets & Samplers* was finished, also my grateful thanks to Nicholas for the computer charts. My wonderful mother-in-law, Irene, and father-in-law, Jim, for helping to run Country Yarns and for always being there when I need them (which is usually most of the time!). Cathy Cosgrave for all her help with the business and also Theresa Nimmo. My agent Doreen Montgomery for all her help, advice and wonderful letters. Di Lewis for such wonderful photography. Everyone at David & Charles for interpreting everything so well, especially Vivienne Wells for patiently listening to all my 'thoughts on the matter'.

I would also like to thank the following companies for supplies used in this book: *DMC Creative World*, Pullman Road, Wigston, Leicester LE18 2DY, for Zweigart fabrics, DMC threads and cards. *Framecraft Miniatures Ltd*, 148/150 High Street, Aston, Birmingham B6 4US, for tree ornaments, trinket pots, bookmarks, wooden and brass bell pulls, brass frames, miniature brass bell, jar lacys, spoon and cards. *Craft Creations Ltd*, 1/7, Harpers Yard, Ruskin Road, Tottenham, London N17 8NE, for craft cards (greetings cards with pre-cut mounts). *Jane Greenoff's Inglestone Collection*, Yells Yard, Cirencester Road, Fairford, Glos G17 4BS, for linen band and perforated paper (stitching paper). *S & A Frames*, 12, Humber Street, Cleethorpes, Humberside DN35 8NN, for the round frame. *C.M.Offray & Sons Ltd*, Fir Tree Place, Church Road, Ashford, Middlesex TW15 2PH, for ribbons. Framing is by *Falcon Art Supplies*, Unit 7, Sedgley Park Trading Estate, George Street, Prestwich, Manchester M25 8WD. Specialist shiny, silk and metallic threads are from *Silken Strands*, 33, Linksway, Gatley, Cheadle, Cheshire SK8 4LA. The hatbox is from *Hatboxes by Jacqueline*, 1, Oakfield Place, Clifton, Bristol BS8 2BJ. General needlecraft supplies are from *Hepatica*, 82a Water Lane, Wilmslow, Cheshire SK9 5BB and *Voirrey Embroidery*, Brimstage Hall, Wirral, Cheshire L63 6JA. When writing to any of the above suppliers, please include a stamped addressed envelope for your reply.

At the time of going to press all threads and materials recommended in this book are available: however, should at some future date this not be the case, the author would always be happy to suggest alternatives if the reader cares to write to her via, *Country Yarns*, Holly Tree House, Lichfield Drive, Prestwich, Manchester M25 8HX.

INDEX

Numbers in *italic* indicate illustrations